*f*P

Beginner's Grace

Bringing Prayer to Life

KATE BRAESTRUP

FREE PRESS
New York   London   Toronto   Sydney

FREE PRESS
A Division of Simon & Schuster, Inc.
1230 Avenue of the Americas
New York, NY 10020

First Free Press hardcover edition November 2010

FREE PRESS and colophon are trademarks of Simon & Schuster, Inc.

For information about special discounts for bulk purchases,
please contact Simon & Schuster Special Sales at
1-866-506-1949 or business@simonandschuster.com.

The Simon & Schuster Speakers Bureau can bring authors to your live event.
For more information or to book an event, contact the Simon & Schuster Speakers Bureau
at 1-866-248-3049 or visit our website at www.simonspeakers.com.

Manufactured in the United States of America

1   3   5   7   9   10   8   6   4   2

Library of Congress Cataloging-in-Publication Data
Braestrup, Kate.
Beginner's grace : bringing prayer to life / Kate Braestrup.—1st
Free Press hardcover ed.
p.   cm.
1. Prayer—Unitarian Universalist Association.   I. Title.
BV215.B69 2010
248.3'2—dc22   2010014725
ISBN 978-1-4391-8426-4
ISBN 978-1-4391-8428-8 (ebook)

Note to Readers: Names and identifying details of some of the persons portrayed in this
book have been changed. In addition, in some instances characters are composites.

To my children:
Erin, Zachary, Peter, Cobus,
Ellie, Ilona, Woolie.
You are my answered prayers.

Contents

Contents

PART ONE

Invitation

1

An Invitation to Prayer

"The nurse said *what*?" I asked.

It was after midnight, but I was already out of bed, groping sleepily for a shirt and a pair of pants.

"Something's wrong." On the other end of the phone, Ruth's voice quavered. "The baby isn't breathing properly."

Ruth was thirty-nine years old and highly educated. She had given birth that afternoon to her third child after a difficult and perhaps not altogether welcome pregnancy.

She had already struggled through one major bout of depression, was having severe back pain from an old injury, and was overwhelmed by the demands of her two small boys. On top of this, she had an emotionally demanding job working with abused children. Because of her medical conditions and "advanced age," her pregnancy was considered high-risk, which meant she had to drive two hours to a specialist every week for prenatal care.

Still, the day before, when I had bumped into Ruth at the community pool, she had seemed pretty upbeat. The water was entertaining her children and helping to support the weight of her belly, and as we chatted, she cheerfully told me that she thought she might already be in early labor.

Baby Nina was born that afternoon by cesarean section, and all had apparently gone well. The other children and Ruth's husband, Wally, had come for a visit and then gone home. That was when, Ruth told me, things started to get strange. The baby wasn't responding well to tests; her oxygen levels were lower than they should have been. Ruth was told that Nina would have to be taken to the neonatal intensive care nursery for a more extensive evaluation. The nurse who escorted Ruth back to her hospital room was silent while Ruth climbed into bed. On her way out, the nurse turned in the doorway and regarded Ruth for a moment.

"And then she told me to pray," Ruth said.

With clumsy, sleepy fingers, I was fitting a white vinyl tab into the collar of my black shirt. The white parallelogram it made at my throat would declare me as clergy.

"Oh, Ruth," I said.

"She said that was my job right now," Ruth went on. "To pray for my baby girl. I'm really sorry to wake you up in the middle of the night, but I don't know what she meant. I don't even know how to pray . . . and I thought maybe, because you're . . . you know, a minister . . . maybe you could just tell me, like, really quickly: How do I pray for my baby?"

"I'll be right there," I said.

I am ordained in a particular form of ministry known as "community ministry." I don't serve in a church, but rather, along with a growing company of clergy, I serve diverse populations out "in the world." Some of us spend our time among the homeless, others as chaplains serving in the military, in hospitals, or with firefighters, police officers, and other first responders. As chaplain to the Maine Warden Service, the agency that polices the state's roughly seventeen million acres of wildland, I accompany game wardens to accidents and drownings and search-and-rescue operations in the Maine woods. Regardless of the circumstances, community ministry brings us into close contact with people whose socioeconomic and religious backgrounds vary widely, and who may share with us little more than birth, illness, and death—the common features of human experience. Whatever theological or doctrinal systems a chaplain begins his ministry with, the work itself has a distinctly streamlining effect. A chaplain doesn't have a leisurely hour in which to explain God. The suffering is right there, and its urgency demands an immediate response. We don't give a lot of sermons out in the field or in the woods or streets. Instead, we are called upon to offer the spiritual equivalent of triage. We're asked to pray.

Arriving at the hospital's neonatal nursery, I expected to see a desperately sick little creature in an incubator. Instead, Nina was stretching and kicking her newborn legs, a lively, lovely baby girl, while a doctor in a white lab coat pressed a stethoscope to her stout little chest. In fact, despite the initially worrying signs, Nina turned out to be fine.

So what on earth was that nurse thinking? To tell the mother of a newborn "You should pray," can only be interpreted as "Your baby is in terrible, terrible trouble." Was the nurse an insensitive religious wacko?

No. She was a human being who had just made a mistake. Among the medicines Ruth had taken for her back pain was methadone. When the nurse reviewed Ruth's file after the baby seemed to have trouble breathing, she saw the drug and jumped to the wrong conclusion: She had thought that Ruth was a heroin addict who had traveled to Bangor, where there is a methadone clinic, throughout her pregnancy.

This isn't really an excuse for psychological cruelty, but it is an explanation: The nurse thought she was dealing with (yet another) substance abuser whose bad choices were inflicting harm on her own helpless offspring. I have felt the same frustration when witnessing catastrophic parental failures in my work as a chaplain.

I could leave it at that—Ruth had been the victim of misdirected and inappropriate anger. She wasn't responsible for her baby's troubles, which, in any case, had proved both mild and transient. Ruth didn't need to pray. Except that she did need to pray. The nurse's exhortations, right or wrong, had triggered an instinctive reaction. What's more, Ruth *wanted* to pray but didn't know how.

So I helped Ruth to pray. Here is the prayer we offered together.

HOSPITAL PRAYER

O God, whose name is love
I offer the prayer of my yearning heart
I can't hold or heal my child.
Please, hold her for me.
Love moves in the skilled hands of those who would heal my
    baby
Love is in their learning and their care
God be in my understanding.
God be in my patience
God be in my arms, as she is returned to me.
May my child and all children be blessed
My family and all families blessed
May God's love enfold us, dwell in us, give us comfort
And grant us peace.
Amen.
    KB

When I invented this Hospital Prayer, more or less on the spot for Ruth and Nina, I drew it from a well that I'd spent years digging. There was a time when I would have imagined that, having dug my well, I could also claim credit for the water.

Why would it occur to Ruth to pray, and how would she know how to do it? Like Ruth's family, my family of origin did not pray and only rarely went to church. I learned enough about religion to be politely silent when prayers were offered at the services I visited with friends and at weddings or funerals. The same culture that taught me both "The Battle Hymn of the Republic" and "Glory! Glory! Hallelujah, Teacher hit me with a ruler" taught me the words of the Lord's Prayer, but it never occurred to me to actually say it. That is, to *pray* it.

In my early twenties, I felt an unfocused longing—not new but never so acute—that made itself known to me through the insistent if prosaic passions of a young woman who took herself and her life very (and probably too) seriously: the intensity of my love for my husband, the moment when another human being gave his first flutter of greeting from deep within my body, and then in the bloody drama of childbirth.

I wanted to name the longing and respond somehow to its source, by some magnificent gesture if possible, but at least with a moment's deliberate attention. No nurse was around to tell me that what I wanted was to pray.

I was of two minds about prayer—correction: I was of more than two minds. I had a whole crowd inside my skull, all jabbering away and no one listening.

Do I have to kneel? Why can't I pray just as well in the shower? Is there anyone to pray to other than the anachronistic God of oily televangelists and creeps? (Here's the church, here's the steeple, open the door, and cheat all the people . . .) Praying on my knees is humiliating, especially when I'm kneeling on a carpet that was probably made by Nepalese teenagers, working their tiny fingers to the bone without even a boom box to make the weary hours fly. What am I supposed to do with my hands? Really, I should get off the floor and make supper or something . . .

This is an example of what the Buddha called "the monkey mind": the running stream-of-consciousness commentary that is the opposite of the clear, calm, contemplative mindfulness a person is supposed to have when she is praying. Right?

I always thought so. And because my mind was never empty, never clear, *jibber jabber jibber jabber*, I couldn't conjure even a moment's meditative mood, which made me feel inadequate and therefore huffy. Untangling myself from the lotus position after trying to meditate, or hoisting myself from the pew after trying to pray, I would self-righteously declare that it was more important to *do* something useful for the Poor and Downtrodden than to sit around praying.

In short, mindfulness with its moments of attention (let alone a magnificent gesture) turned out to be a tall order for my mind, which was well stuffed with both the concerns of new motherhood and the details of everyday life. There were immunization appointments, the Iran-Contra fiasco, grocery lists, Penelope Leach vs. Dr. Spock, the oil bill, a freelance editing job, my husband's state police uniforms to pick up at the dry cleaner, and a child's persistent need for a fresh diaper.

Prayer was already present and available to me in more ways than I realized. Saying grace before a meal or a prayer at bedtime was familiar to me from visits to friends' houses and from books and other media, even if my family didn't engage in it. On the face of it, prayer seemed harmless enough to try, just for the heck of it. The major obstacle for me was ignorance: I really didn't understand what prayer was. I had thought that conquering the monkey mind and bringing myself into a conscious attentiveness were prerequisites for prayer, but they are not: They are prayer's *result*. If I was restless, dubious, and distracted whenever I'd try to pray, so what? Everyone is!

What keeps you from prayer?

Ask that question in a roomful of people who don't pray, and you will get a raft of answers: Oh, I'm too busy. I'm uncomfortable. All the people I know who pray are real jerks, and I don't want to be one of them. I have bad memories of abusive religious figures. I wouldn't know who I was praying to. I don't know what to say.

Here and there one comes across that true rarity, a person who is wholly neutral when it comes to prayer, but most people have strong opinions, at least about when, how, and to whom we would rather *not* pray. We don't want to be forced to pray in the forms and words of a religion we don't subscribe to, or to a God we don't believe in. So we don't pray at all, and life moves along in its busy, mindless, distracted way until an eighteen-wheeler is veering over the double line into our lane and life is suddenly very simple.

This is a book about bringing true prayer to real life, preferably before real life includes an eighteen-wheeler or other looming disaster. I won't claim that prayer can get you a new car or find the lover of your dreams. It won't help you gain status, assert your dominance, or otherwise please your ego. It won't even make life easier.

What it can do—what prayer, at its best and at *our* best, has always done—is help us to live consciously, honorably, and compassionately. Because I am not stronger, more self-sufficient, smarter, braver, or any less mortal than my forebears or my neighbors, I need this help. As long as prayer helps me to be more loving, then I need prayer. As long as prayer serves as a potent means of sharing my love with others, I need prayer.

There are many ways to pray and many reasons to choose one way over another. These we will explore in the pages ahead. There are also plenty of sources to draw on if the prayers included here don't seem quite right.

Since I am a minister in the Protestant tradition, you might expect me to recommend reading the Bible from cover to cover before you do anything else. Well, I tried that strategy back in the day. I made a pretty good start in the Garden of Eden. Then, like so many others, I got bogged down in the "begats"—the seemingly endless genealogies of Genesis 10.

Perhaps there are people who can chomp their way straight through the duller bits of the Bible and extract a spiritual awakening from the (let's face it) pretty weird and violent stories that make up the more interesting parts. Maybe there are those so attuned to the Word that they can crack open the Bible and have both faith and practice all sussed out by the middle of Second Kings. If so, I'm not among them. I have been wrestling with this complex, infuriating, wonderful, awful text in various ways for nearly thirty years now, and though the Book holds blessings, they didn't yield themselves easily.

Books on spiritual practice and prayer are generally aimed at specific audiences—Buddhists, Christians, Jews, recovering alcoholics, or willing believers who need extra help with a specific problem. When I began having my own barely articulated questions about prayer, I didn't fit into any of these categories.

There were plenty of churches and other religious institutions in the neighborhood that would have been pleased to take me in, but I thought I knew all about Organized Religion. At least I knew enough to know I didn't want anything to do with it.

I wasn't seeking to become Catholic, Methodist, or Jewish. I couldn't picture myself attending weekly services, joining a choir, and organizing the rummage sale. The strange, restless longing that compelled my search was still too fresh to name with what I thought of as the usual depleted words—"God," for example. I just wanted to respond to it—and to life around me—without feeling false or foolish. I didn't want someone to tell me what to *be* (Episcopalian! Saved!). I needed someone to tell me what to *do*.

Finally, of course, someone did.

I was going through a miserable time. It was probably postpartum depression. Naturally, I concealed my distress, and I thought I was doing so successfully. Then I ran into Pastor Larry, a large, gray-bearded retired Methodist minister, an experienced hospital chaplain with a lovely, deep, rumbling Hebrew Patriarch sort of voice. I recognized that voice immediately, even before I saw him, as it carried from the other side of the self-help stack at Second Read Books in Rockland, Maine (now known as Rock City Books & Coffee), where I was browsing. Feminist though I am, on that unhappy day, "patriarchal" didn't seem all that negative a quality. In fact, if I could have gotten away with it, I would've crawled into his lap—Father! Abba!—and bawled. Instead, I said, "Hello! How are you?"

Pastor Larry looked at me from under his luxuriant gray eyebrows. Then he calmly announced he was going to write me a prescription.

Rooting around in his jacket pockets, he unearthed an old envelope and a ballpoint pen. Mystified, I watched him write. Because his enormous left hand completely engulfed and concealed the envelope, I couldn't actually see the words. There seemed to be an awful lot of them.

"There," Larry said at last. He folded the paper in half. "Twice a day," he said, holding it out to me. "More, if necessary."

I unfolded the paper. Larry had written out the Twenty-third Psalm.

Faith is so often the attitude of last resort. I could not imagine an end to my unhappiness, let alone conjure words that could describe or assuage it. I bowed my head. "Okay," I said. "Thank you."

And so the atheist in her foxhole prayed the Twenty-third Psalm about ten times a day. I could have recited it—I soon knew the thing by heart—but I didn't. Taking the paper out of my pocket, unfolding it carefully, and seeing Larry's handwriting was the most comforting aspect of the ritual. Later, when life began to improve a bit, I realized that the paper, the handwriting, and my mental image of Pastor Larry's kind, fatherly face were of a piece with the psalm.

The Lord is my shepherd, I shall not want.
He makes me lie down in green pastures;
He leads me beside still waters;
He restores my soul.
He leads me in right paths for His name's sake.

Even though I walk through the darkest valley,
I fear no evil;
for you art with me;
your rod and your staff–
they comfort me.

You prepare a table before me
in the presence of my enemies;
you anoint my head with oil;
my cup overflows.
Surely goodness and mercy shall follow me
all the days of my life,

and I shall dwell in the house of the Lord
my whole life long.
Psalm 23

Although he called the psalm a "prescription," Larry didn't actually make any healing claims for prayer. A variety of religions do lay claim to miraculous abilities to cure all manner of human ills through prayer or other rituals, from obesity to cancer. Some say they are able to personally persuade or even require the Deity du Jour to give us riches, affection, safety, and thin thighs and take away our loneliness, bad weather, enemies, or acne—*poof!*—just like that.

Alternatively, religious practice can be made to sound like a recreational drug. "Melt one tab of prayer under your tongue, and you shall visualize whirled peas and angels dancing on the head of a pin. Take two tabs, and Trinitarian theory will make sense, and thou shalt be able to read the begats without boredom . . ."

Prayer is sometimes offered to us coated with a scientific gloss: It exercises our body's cells in specific ways, it is said, or it is a way to lasso and harness a powerful but furtive energy and turn it to our own ends. I am not a new ager or a mystic. I've neither conjured visions of the Virgin nor, to the best of my knowledge, vanquished even a single pimple by praying.

Even now that I am a chaplain, my expectations for prayer are pretty low. Though sometimes moved to spontaneous prayer by an experience of the sacred (sacred sorrow or sacred joy), more often I pray because I have committed myself to it as a practice or because it's my job. So what remains the most surprising fact about prayer for me is that it consistently exceeds my expectations.

It works.

Just as long as I have breath
I must answer yes to life
Though with pain I made my way
Still with hope I meet each day

If they ask what I did well
Tell them I said yes to life.
Just as long as vision lasts
I must answer yes to truth
In my dream and in my dark
Always that elusive spark
If they ask what I did well
Tell them I said yes to truth.
Just as long as my heart beats
I must answer yes to love
Disappointment pierced me through
Still I kept on loving you.
If they ask what I did best
Tell them I said yes to love.

2

The Starting Point

My slender lemon-tree seedling pulls herself from the soil I tucked with care about her heel. As though stung from beneath, as if that soil contained some irritant, she holds her little seed leaves high, like fists: a scrapper! Fighting her way up from a paper cup to the light that is not Florida's but suffices.

I don't know why I think of her—of it—as a girl. I never expected the seed, which I'd sown absentmindedly, to sprout, let alone to grow, let alone to become a growing thing that moves my heart.

"You are the instant of a tree," I say aloud, enraptured. She is a wisp in a cup, one of her two leaves sporting the seed shell still. And then I say my prayers.

I begin with a bad attitude. My body is restless, my heart is troubled, and doubt blooms vigorously in the fertile soil of my modern monkey mind. Oh yes, it's still there, shrilly suggesting a dozen more amusing and productive activities I could be engaged in. Why pray? Why pray?

The Lord is my shepherd, I shall not want . . .

If there is a problem in my life—and there always is—my mind jabbers away, trying to solve it, and won't easily yield the floor.

He maketh me to lie down in green pastures: he leadeth me beside the still waters. He restoreth my soul . . .

What if you do . . . what if you say . . . what if you ask . . . what if you try . . . so many excellent suggestions the monkey mind makes! Maybe I should go get a pencil to write down these brilliant ideas before I lose them?

He leadeth me in the paths of righteousness for his name's sake . . .

Oh, but there it is. The leading edge of that little wave of . . . what? The monkey mind begins to slow and slur, the way I do when Pam, at the hair salon, massages my scalp before a haircut.

I will fear no evil: for thou art with me . . .

"Thou art with me": Pastor Larry says that this is the most important line in the psalm. ("You don't have to do it alone," he would rumble. Dear old Pastor Larry.)

Surely goodness and mercy shall follow me all the days of my life . . .

Nothing in the material world has changed, the monkey points out drowsily. It's true. If I was generally content with life before I began to pray, I'm still content. If life sucked, it sucketh still.

And I will dwell in the house of the Lord forever.

I have read and studied prayer. I've developed various theories and opinions about it. But I learned what I needed to know about prayer by doing it. So this book begins not with beliefs but with *practice*. I will describe the times, places, and prayers that are part of my own and my family's daily life, and I'll explain why these seem to me to be useful and effective. Written prayers are sprinkled throughout the book (and all are listed in the appendix as well).

Long ago, my husband and I lay side by side, not touching but companionable, in a room in my mother's house with all the windows open.

Outside, on a spring-wet day, water ran clear from the sky. It ran across from the glass in the windows and down the pine board walls where it had blown in. We smelled pine boards, shellac, and wet grass.

He pointed out the hillside where the horses stood, dark across their backs and streaked dark around their bellies where the water rolled. They shuffled their soft noses in the clover and shook like dogs when the rain dripped into their ears.

"The windows are full of green," my husband said.

Prime viridian, a shimmer of lime above the wet-black trunk of the plum tree, the dark wet fur of the pines, the pale fiddleheads, all that grass.

"Any seed could grow today," he said. "I have an urge to plant."

Later, in a winter moving fast toward a drier spring, I heard the baby move beneath my heart. It was more sound than sensation: I listened for him.

He is alone, I thought. *And I am never alone now.*

Planted, my baby grew in a vessel of rainwater under my heart, safe within the shell of my own bones, given.

The beginning of my prayer.

At a family dinner party in 1986, very pregnant with my first child, I felt the baby turn over. His weight shifted from one side of my body to the other, and I thought: *There are nine, not eight, people at this table. Hidden by a mere inch or two of skin, muscle, and membrane, there's another human being, as individual and alive as I am.*

If I had mentioned this to my relatives, they probably would have been interested, if not quite as excited about it as my husband and I. But then they were all drinking wine. I was virtuously sticking to water, and since one of the two I was eating for was my own baby and I already loved him (though I thought for sure I was carrying a girl), I was careful to avoid any substance deemed harmful and to take in enough of the right nutrients. My son Zachary was being knit together, his inward parts being formed, my body building his flesh from my flesh, his bone from my bone. My child would have what he needed for life, poured through the placenta to a new heart, built and beating.

A couple of months later, having taken that strange, brief, strenuous journey into the startling fact of air, my hungry, bewildered boy took a breath and squalled. I immediately put him to my breast. "Take. Eat," his mother said, and so he did.

However miraculous his parents thought him at that moment, in this Zachary was like all the millions of human babies before and since, and all the millions and billions of mammalian cubs, calves, pups, kits, fawns, and foals: all those suckling little mouths going back to the pink maw of the first tiny rodent that scuttled past the feet of the dinosaurs.

And my son was just like Jesus, who, as a fully human infant, was likewise given his mother's body, his mother's blood, and then his mother's breast. "Take. Eat," said Mary. "This is my body which is given for you."

"Truly, I tell you, unless you change and become like children, you will never enter the kingdom of heaven," Jesus said to his disciples.

If my firstborn child was setting an example for prayer, he was a Holy Roller, praising, inviting the Spirit to come down. He spoke in tongues—*gau-oooh! gau-oooh!*—and his crib would shake.

When I reached my hands—*oh, yes! praise be!*—down to him, I was *Salvation! Holy, holy.* He was uplifted whole. *Hallelujah! She is come!*

With his devoted mouth he'd suckle on. His jaw would work in a rhythm as old or older than the sixth day: *Oh, and it was good!* His hands were folded, one to another, over his beating heart, and with every greedy draw, he prayed:

Milk, oh, milk, milk.

My mother-in-law says that all prayer and any prayer begins with "yes" and ends with "thank you." Zachary's prayers certainly did. And he prayed a lot, from Lauds to Compline, with special attention paid to the Night Office, or Matins.

When Brooklyn-born Franciscan priest Father Mychal Judge had the honor of meeting Mother Teresa during one of her New York visits, he asked her for some spiritual advice.

The saintly nun, in effect, told him to pray the way a newborn infant nurses: often, long, and round the clock. She advised a total prayer time of at least two hours a day. Taken aback, Father Mychal replied in his strong Brooklyn accent: "Well, sure, but I gotta get ta' work, ya' know . . ."

If prayer is "yes, please" and "thank you," is saying grace before a meal just a part of etiquette? When dining with God, you've got to use the right spoon for the right course and hold your pinkie in the air while you drink your tea, right? Actually, manners are more often remnant prayers. "Goodbye" is a contracted descendant of "God be with you," and sneezing (into the crook of your elbow, please) remains a way to solicit blessings from a group.

There are some polite traditions that we have learned to live without. For instance, it was once considered mannerly to leave a little food on one's plate at the end of the meal, as a treat (!?) for the person who would clear the dishes—in the same spirit, I guess, that ancient farmers would leave a bit of grain in the fields after the harvest for the impoverished to glean. These days we prefer a living wage and food stamps. Still, the impulse is the same: Manners are accepted signifiers of recognition, care, and respect.

As signifiers, they can vary, and we don't even have to drag up the example that it is considered polite to belch at the table in China (so often cited as a defense by prepubescent children!). If you are walking down the street in small-town Maine, it's normal to meet the eyes of passersby and offer a greeting. But we consider downtown Thomaston thronged if we find ourselves offering those polite hellos to twenty strangers over the course of a day—there are only a little more than a million people in the whole state, after all. On a street in Manhattan, one can easily be faced with twenty people in as many seconds. That much incidental social contact is simply exhausting, and because New Yorkers don't want to wear one another out, they do the polite thing and keep their eyes and their greetings to themselves.

If a lapsed Whatever refrains from prayer, he or she might be able to justify it on the grounds of good New York City manners. If you imagine God as a humanoid deity (resembling the earnest Morgan Freeman rather than the insouciant George Burns) who is expected to listen to and answer—in some way, however mysterious—the prayers of six billion human tongues, sheer pity would move any polite person to restrain himself from all but the "Oh God oh God oh God" prayers of dire and immediate crisis.

Population density isn't the only cause of variations in our manners. One of the distinctive cultural differences that our Brazilian exchange student, Olivia, noticed when she arrived in the United States was that Americans thank everybody. Back in Brazil, a waiter in an upscale São Paulo restaurant might expect a thank-you, but the guy behind the counter at a fast-food restaurant will not. Olivia thinks the phenomenon arises out of the ways each country deals with social class. In Brazil, she says, manners are what the inferior owe to the superior. The inferior yields room on the sidewalk or a seat on the bus, lowers her eyes, doffs his hat.

In the United States, we are attached to the idea that we are all free and equal, even if in practice some are, as George Orwell would say, "more equal than others."

Whether in America or Brazil, the McDonald's fry cook may not have a realistic alternative to serving a wealthier customer her meal, but in America, we are doggedly committed to the fiction that she does. We acknowledge her freedom by saying, "I'd like some french fries, [if you] please." After she has freely chosen to give us our french fries, we thank her for her choice.

When we say "please" and "thank you" to the waiter who brought our meal, Granny who presented us with a nice necktie, or the cardiologist who performed our triple bypass, we are implicitly accepting that the person who has served us had a choice about whether to do so. While presumably any God worth the title has a real choice about whether to bless a sneezer or keep our departing guests company ("Goodbye!"), mere courteous appreciation seems a dry, unsatisfying rationale for prayer.

If refraining from prayer altogether can be considered snobbish and ungrateful, praying without gratitude is, as Francis "Crazy Love" Chan puts it, "serving leftovers to God." Genuine gratitude, the gratitude of prayer, must ultimately arise out of a profound recognition that *things could be other than what they are.*

If you will forgive a small diversion into a kind of mysticism—things could *not be*. At all.

The true realist should expect what is most likely. That which is most likely is nothing. "Nothing is impossible!" people say, but actually, everything *except* nothing is impossible. Nothingness is the most possible—indeed, the most *probable*—thing in the cosmos. Not only is there no inevitability involved when the fry cook gives you your french fries, the odds are a bazillion to one against either of you (or the potatoes) existing at all.

Yet here you are!

And here I am! *How cool is this?*

I can't thank myself for the impossible fact of my existence. With all due respect, I can't thank you for it, either. Maybe I don't have to thank anyone for it—but I am thankful, dammit! And I'm sure it's bad for my blood pressure to keep all that thankfulness bottled up inside.

If, as my husband defines it, disappointment is the feeling you get when reality doesn't meet your expectations, gratitude is the feeling you get when reality *exceeds* your expectations. The truly rational, realistic person should feel overwhelmingly grateful all the time.

The Psalms of the Hebrew Scriptures contain lavish expressions of gratitude to God: *I will extol you, O Lord, for you have drawn me up, and did not let my foes rejoice over me . . . O Lord my God, I cried to you for help, and you have healed me . . . Sing praises to the Lord, O you his faithful ones, and give thanks to his holy name . . . O Lord my God, I will give thanks to you forever.*

If you think of gratitude as the disagreeable task of the inferior who "owes" the superior, reading the lavish praise of the Psalmist is uncomfortable, like overhearing an abused spouse cringing before an irascible mate in the hope of forestalling a blow.

True gratitude isn't cringing or uncomfortable at all: It is the purest expression of joy. Ungrateful people—you may have met a few—are not happy people. If we humans were making good use of our consciousness, we would wander around in a flabbergasted daze of gratitude all the time: *I could be hungry . . . but instead, I've got french fries! There could be nothing . . . but instead, there's something!*

There could be only birth, pain, and death. Instead, there is also love.

St. Francis of Assisi, who really did walk around in flabbergasted gratitude all the time, wrote: *Such love does the sky now pour, that whenever I stand in a field, I have to wring the light out when I get home.*

Wouldn't you like to wring the light out of your clothes at the end of another normal, hectic day? Maybe it is because I am American, but bowing my head or even flinging myself down into that puddle of grace and praying *thank you, thank you, thank you* doesn't seem silly or irrational. Indeed, it strikes me as the most reasonable response possible for anyone faced with the impossible facts of a good meal, love, and even being.

> Sing praises of the Lord with heart and soul
> Singing heart, embrace the spirit
> The notes play, like the stars that sparkle
> Joyously around the name of the Lord.
>   N. F. S. Grundtvig

3

Beginning with Grace

I don't pray two hours a day, but I do pray daily. As an infant, I doubtless prayed as frantically before my meals as anyone— perhaps more so, since old photographs show a pasty blob with a greedy look in her beady little eyes. As an adult, I also began my formal prayer life with a prayer before a meal, and thus literally began with grace. My children and I were sharing Thanksgiving with friends, and since I had contributed nothing substantive to the meal, I offered to say grace. Unfortunately, I realized too late that I didn't know any graces. So I made one up on the spot.

> We are thankful for the food
> And for the hands that prepared it
> And for our family and for our friends.
> Amen.

Assuming we're at home, seated around the table, we close our eyes and hold hands to say it. It's simple, easy for the kids' friends to learn, and brief enough that a new guest doesn't have to indulge our religiosity for long.

Over a meal of take-out sushi, my visiting brother responded to our grace with a derisive snort. "Are we thankful for the hands of the Japanese guys at the sushi restaurant?"

23

Immediately, I pictured slender hands, precisely arranging maki rolls, wasabi, and shards of pale pickled ginger on a tray. "Yes," I answered, but I didn't need to, for as soon as he had asked the question, my brother felt the answer for himself: *We are thankful for the sushi, the hands of the Japanese guys at the restaurant, the fishermen, the rice farmers, the makers of soy sauce* . . . Gratitude isn't so hard to conjure once you've given it room to appear and expand.

Since my husband does most of the cooking, the hands that prepare it are usually his. (It is not hard for me, at least, to feel truly thankful for Simon's hands.) Our grace often seems too brief and candid to be a prayer. Still, it works like one. No matter how harassed I am, how annoyed with my kids or distracted by my work, I can close my eyes, grasp the grubby paws on either side, recite those twenty-two words, and my spirit returns from its fretful wanderings and comes gratefully home to the small human community of my family.

Born into a Catholic family, my husband, Simon, grew up saying this grace before meals:

Bless us, O Lord and these thy gifts
Which we are about to receive from Thy bounty
Through Christ our Lord.
Amen.

I have also heard a version that is both shorter and suitable for meals attended by those of differing traditions: *For these Thy gifts, which we are about to enjoy, may we be truly thankful.*

My son Zach must have come across that one, too, because when he was asked to say grace before another Thanksgiving meal, he bowed his head and, with every appearance of piety, intoned: "'For these thy gifts which we are about to endure, may we be truly thankful.'" (This earned him a gratifying squawk from our hostess, his great-aunt Harriet.)

Because he is a gracious man, Simon goes along with the grace my children and I made up. When supper is to be served in some scattered way—as a buffet, for example, or in the car on the way to soccer practice—or even if we're so hungry that twenty-two words are about eighteen more than our empty bellies are willing to wait for, he will sometimes offer a modest "Blessings on this food." It suffices. We eat.

This grace, given me by one of the Book Babes of Montpelier, Vermont, is another good variation:

> For the food before us
> And the friends beside us
> And the love that surrounds us
> We are truly grateful.
> Anonymous

"If I teach my child a specific prayer, I'll be indoctrinating her in a particular religion," a young man objected, enfolding his three-year-old protectively in his arms. "I want Eleanor to be free to choose her own beliefs."

Parents in twentieth- and twenty-first-century Western cultures are faced with a peculiar problem. We revere freedom, especially freedom of conscience. All freedom rests upon the freedom to choose not only among various actions but also between competing ideas.

Is the parent who inculcates a helpless child with specific ideas about the nature and meaning of reality trying to limit her freedom of conscience and control her thought? And, Eleanor's young father asked me, if he were to insist that his daughter recite a pre-scribed set of words at specific time of day, wouldn't this be sort of Stalinesque?

Eleanor's father obviously loves his child. He is thoughtful, educated, and conscientious. He is also glumly aware that our consumer culture is doing its noisy best to persuade children that food should be brightly colored, extremely sweet, and incredibly convenient. It was not hard to get him to admit that, no, he would not put a bowl of vegetable stew next to a bowl of Cap'n Crunch and let his daughter freely choose between them. Because he wants Eleanor to drink more milk than soda, because he is hoping her little palate will learn to prefer foods that are healthful, nutritious, and flavorful, Eleanor's father and mother not only don't allow her to choose but, to the extent possible, restrict her access to "information" about what the choices are. (That is, Eleanor's parents don't let her watch television.)

When Eleanor is an adult, it will be up to her to decide whether to floss her teeth, eat her vegetables, or watch twelve back-to-back episodes of *Dexter*. She will also be free to smoke dope, starve herself to fashion-model thinness, hook up with strangers, or use racial slurs. She can choose whether to clean her body, her house, or the environment, whether to help the poor or ignore them, say "please" and "thank you" or take the service of others for granted. In the meantime, as lovingly yet authoritatively as they can, her parents make these choices for her.

If they do not train Eleanor to like broccoli, the world will happily train her to love Skittles. If they don't give her tools and practices for interpreting and expressing the universal human need for meaningful communion and a sense of purpose, the world will happily fill the void ("you spin my head right round, right round, when you go down, when you go down").

"Katie," my piano teacher told me when I was about fourteen, "how you practice is how you play. It's up to you. You can practice to play the piano. Or you can practice to *not* play the piano."

I was bored with Bach minuets and those infernal Béla Bartók exercises, composed especially to foil people like me, who played by ear.

I chose to practice *not* playing the piano. Unsurprisingly, I can't play now.

How you practice is how you play, but human beings are adaptable creatures. We can take a skill we learned when applying it to one thing and figure out how to apply it to something else. Practicing Bach, in the long term, would have allowed me to play any music I wished to—Joplin, Coltrane, the Beatles, or Norah Jones.

Refusing to practice Bach narrowed my choices down to one: I listen. (Often to Bach, ironically enough.)

Children brought up on fast food are likely to be gastronomically handicapped, yet even these benighted little ones will nonetheless have their own choices to make when they're grown—at least if they're lucky enough to remain in a world of abundant choice. The starving, on the other hand, are left with only one choice.

"To the hungry, God's love can only reveal itself in the form of bread," Gandhi said.

Sacred foods and ritual meals are so common a feature of religious life that it hardly seems worth explaining that food serves as a deep, abiding source of sacred metaphor because it, like air, water, and sleep, is immediately necessary to life. My family (and probably yours) is in the extraordinary position of being part of the first society in history in which our most pressing widespread health problems are caused by consuming too many calories rather than too few. For millennia, and for too many of our brothers and sisters today, hunger is the first pain and the final agony of human life. The hungry, therefore, have no problem whatever grasping the sacredness of food.

This is expressed in the fasts of Ramadan and Lent, the feasts of Eid ul-Fitr and Easter. Food's sacred meanings are also expressed through the quotidian feasts and fasts of various dietary restrictions: no bacon, no shellfish, no two-toed beasts; Fridays taste like flounder, and Rosh Hashanah like apples and honey.

For Christians, the most familiar sacred meal is the Last Supper, the meal Jesus shared with his disciples on the night before he was to be taken away and crucified. In the midst of that part of the story known as the Passion, Jesus joins his friends for the Passover feast. He holds up a loaf of bread, blesses it, and breaks it. *[He] gave it to the disciples, and said, "Take, eat: this is my body." Then he took a cup, and after giving thanks he gave it to them, saying, "Drink from it, all of you; for this is my blood . . ."* (Matthew 26–29)

Non-Christians might be forgiven for regarding this as a distinctly unappetizing invitation to cannibalism, while Christians of various stripes seem to enjoy debating whether Jesus meant that the bread was *metaphorically* his body or *literally* his body, and if the latter, what was it that was sitting there talking, blessing, and eating? If blessed bread is physically Jesus, should a priest avoid growing whiskers lest a bit of his savior get hung up in his mustache?

We can skip such entertainment for now; I'm more interested in the foods Jesus chose to either symbolize or literally become himself when he was no longer visibly present. If we accept that the meal in question was the Passover Feast (Matthew, Mark, and Luke all agree on this point, while John demurs), a variety of foods would have been on the table—a greater variety, that is, than an ordinary meal provided. This was a meal held to celebrate the great transformative moment in Jewish history, the exodus out of slavery in Egypt, and the beginning of the journey to the Promised Land. Whoever was in charge of the menu would have done her best to make it memorable.

Nowadays, at least in the United States, most priests and pastors don't rip whole loaves apart at the altar; neither do they just haul in a few bags of Wonder Bread when it's time for communion. Instead, they purchase little boxes of specially made, easy-to-break unleavened wafers (round or square, wheat, whole wheat, or wheat-free, and pretty costly, pound for pound, unless you wait for a good sale and stock up).

Nor do we Americans drink wine the way people once did. For the people of the ancient world, bread and wine were the most common and, indeed, often the only items they consumed. Bread and wine for breakfast, bread and wine for lunch, bread and wine for dinner, and bread and wine as the basis and the filler for all feasts. Bread and wine were inexpensive and ordinary. Couldn't Jesus (God incarnate, the story goes, and therefore surely a gourmet) declare himself to be spices, pomegranates, meat, or figs, some rarer, more delicious thing more easily recognized as sacred than the foods we tend to gobble down untasted?

Ask the poor, the hungry, the stranger in our midst: Why would

Jesus choose to infuse his sacred self into the cheapest, most ordinary, and easy-to-find food in what was then imagined to be the whole wide world? While you're at it, ask the misfit, the prisoner, or even the naughty child to explain why Judas—already identified as the betrayer of Christ—was also given the bread and wine, the body and blood, the nourishment and the promise?

Jesus offered thanks before he broke the bread—thanks to God, no doubt, but I'll bet he also thanked the person who had baked the bread and poured the wine. Perhaps, being Jesus, he also considered the farmers who scythed the wheat and cut the clusters from the vine, the millers and vintners and those who gathered salt or crushed the olive for its oil.

I don't think it's far-fetched to imagine him acknowledging the gift of the earth itself, broken by the plow and nourished by the rain that poured so the seeds could sprout and the grapes grow plump. Maybe grace, in those days, was a psalm sung gladly, especially as the wine began to have its effect.

> Sing to the LORD with thanksgiving;
> make melody to our God on the lyre.
> He covers the heavens with clouds,
> prepares rain for the earth,
> makes grass grow on the hills.
> He gives to the animals their food,
> and to the young ravens when they cry.
> Psalm 147

My cousin Lise's family sings grace. Her three girls join their parents in a rousing chorus of "The Lord Is Good to Me" before supper every night.

When they were little, they merely sang it, con brio if not exactly tunefully. Now that they are older, the sung grace is often supplemented by a speech on the theme of "things we are grateful for." Because Lise and her husband, Mark, have bright and verbal girls, this sometimes leads to rather lengthy orations, some that spawn debate about what is and is not God's doing (the victory of your softball team? finding your library book under the couch? being accepted at the college of your choice?) or contain subtle insults (as when one daughter gave fervent thanks to God for her sister's laryngitis).

When the premeal homilies begin to wander from the point, one parent or the other will take a loud, deep breath and start singing:

> Oh! The Lord is good to me
> And so I thank the Lord
> For giving me
> The things I need
> The sun and the moon and the apple tree
> The Lord is good to me—YIPPEE!

Offering thanks for a meal is familiar, mannerly, and sensible, so much so that you might overlook the other helpful attribute of mealtime. It occurs with considerable regularity, once, twice, or three times a day, and because even forgetful and preoccupied people generally remember to eat, saying grace before supper doesn't require nearly as much self-discipline as carving out a distinct time for spiritual activity from days that are already overbooked.

Maybe, like the people of the Ancient Near East, you plan to have the grain of the broken earth and fruit of the hanging vine for supper tonight. Or perhaps you're in the mood for Japanese Kobe steak or a bowl of canned beef stew at the Salvation Army food kitchen. Maybe it'll be rice and beans, peanut butter sandwiches, fried tofu with bok choy, or a bowl of cornflakes. Regardless of what it is, every morsel of food we put into our mouth is a blessing. Saying grace doesn't make it into a blessing; it already is one. Holy Communion isn't the only holy meal, it is the meal that can remind us that every meal is holy.

May the hungry be well fed. May the well fed hunger for justice.
Amen.

4

Prayers in the Dark and Quiet

If you have already begun speaking or singing some appropriate little blessing with your loved one(s) before supper, in this simple way you have already established—*presto!*—a "daily devotional practice."

My fitness instructor (known to her clients as Fräulein Cindy de Sade) informs me cheerfully that the logic of physical fitness is not teleological but tautological. This means that the goal of exercise is to enable you to exercise *more*.

I loathe exercise. I would much rather lie on the couch and read. I can bring myself to work out only by maintaining an irrational faith in a glorious future of unchangeable physical perfection. When that day comes, all the sweat shall be dried and muscle cramps, too, shall pass away. In the blessed state of perfect fitness—free at last!—I shall not have to run another step, nor shall I suffer through one more damned abdominal crunch.

I would protest more strenuously, if no more efficaciously, to Cindy's faith-shattering pronouncement were it not for the fact that prayer works exactly the same way. There will be no moment—in this life, anyway—when I will be able to say, "That's it! I've prayed, and the prayers have paid off: I'm a fully conscious, totally grateful, and unstintingly generous person. I can just start stuffing myself as soon as the plate hits the table."

As far as physical fitness goes, science writer Natalie Angier writes of the good news: Everything in your body heads south (literally, in some instances), but muscle always comes back. Work a muscle and it will respond. Even people well beyond middle age—elderly people—have been found to significantly increase their strength in response to strenuous exercise. Muscle comes back, and the more you work it, the faster it responds. The harder you work it, the stronger you become.

The more you give, the more you will be able to give; the more you receive, the more you will be willing to receive; and the more you pray, the more you can . . . pray.

Uninspiring as my attitude toward fitness might be, it nonetheless illustrates a principle I would offer to lazy pray-ers: A little bit of mindfulness is better than none at all, and a little bit of prayer will eventually allow for a little more.

Prayer doesn't require a church or special equipment any more than fitness requires a gym, though both may one day seem more appealing than they do at the start. All prayer requires is a little time.

"Quiet time," a friend suggested. "And quiet is even harder to find than time. Unless you get up at five in the morning or something." She eyed me suspiciously, as if I were about to suggest such a thing.

I don't get up at five in the morning—at least, not specifically to pray. Sometimes, in my job as Warden Service chaplain, I am asked to be on the other end of the state by 0900 hours, which means I've got to be on the road well before dawn.

Last winter, I was called to Downeast Maine, where the Warden Service dive team would be diving beneath ice for the body of a woman who had gone skating the night before and fallen through. It was dark when I awoke, dark when I left home, and my boots squeaked so loudly on the dry, cold snow of the driveway that I feared awakening my whole family with the noise.

Winter nights are quiet enough for prayer, but I was in the car with the heater roaring, headed down the driveway, my mind busy with route numbers and road names, so I didn't think to offer even a terse blessing to the rearview mirror.

An hour later and forty miles from home, my hair—damp from the shower and frozen crisp in the time it took to scurry the thirty feet from my door to the car—had finally completely thawed. The wheels turned beneath me, accompanied by the familiar, unpleasant grinding noise from the crust of dirt, road salt, and snow that, thrown up by the tires, had formed in the wheel wells where the tires rubbed against them. When I stopped for gas, I'd go around and kick the crust loose, and I was sort of looking forward to this, one of the weird, small satisfactions of a Maine winter.

When I first began working as a chaplain, I would spend the driving time trying to anticipate what might be required of me at a scene. Anxiously, I would rummage through the "pastoral care" files in my head, conjuring what counsel might be appropriate for a snowmobile accident, a missing hunter, or the drowning death of a mother of three. I was so seldom accurate in my predictions that I gave up trying. Now I just drive. When I get there, God will have to figure out what use to make of me.

The road I traveled to get to the scene followed the coast for a time, sometimes skirting the shore so closely that a scrap of ice-glazed turf was all that separated the macadam from the complex geometry of salt-washed granite ledge and cold water. The stone had been chopped and fractured into rectangles and trapezoids by freeze-and-thaw and time (those old, strong, simple tools), and at the water's edge, where wave after wave flung a fine spray, layers of rime had built up until each separate granite block was thickly shrink-wrapped in ice. When the sun came up, the ice-wrapped granite blocks gleamed white, pale aquamarine, and gold.

I pulled the car onto the verge and turned off the motor. I sat gazing at the dark water, rocks wrapped in light from a pale sky. Consumed by a yearning whose object I couldn't identify, I could think of no way to respond to it, though I wanted badly to respond. So I just sat there and let the sun rise.

I would like to be able to say that I soon got my act together and did the obvious thing, composing a splendid prayer and leaping from my warm car to sing it, there beside the frosted road, like

Miriam with her tambourine, singing beside the Red Sea. No. The best I could do was to murmur, inarticulately, "Wow."

Maybe all prayer is composed of three words, not two? Yes. *Wow.* And thanks.

I started the engine and followed the road as it curved away from the coast and began to lead me inland along the tidal river. The sun rose higher. I passed an inlet with big disks of yellowish ice floating like cornflakes in a bowl of blue-white skim milk. Atop one thick flake, an eagle stood on yellow legs, the red rags of some half-devoured creature held fast beneath one claw. The eagle turned and met my gaze with its disdainful yellow eyes.

In a little while, I would reach the place by the river where I'd find the dive team. Even now they were drinking their coffee, hauling oxygen tanks, doing the safety checks on their dive gear.

The brighter light of day revealed thin places, but last night's moonlight had shown the river as a seductive ribbon of pearly ice, opaque and apparently uniform. The ice-skater had sat down on the bank. The seat of her snow pants had made a rounded impression in the snow, and the ends of her blades had left gouges in the ice where she had braced her skates for lacing.

Two lines incised in the ice declared her path to those arriving afterward. Straight and sure, they nearly crossed the river, terminating at a jagged hole that glinted black as obsidian in all that gleaming whiteness.

By the time I arrived, Warden Bruce Loring would already be dressed in his Gumby suit. Clumsy in air, he would slip smoothly into this thick, liquid underworld. There were people waiting in the world above the ice, the ones who longed for the return of the woman's body, that they might care for it and lay it safely to rest.

As the eagle bent its head above its meal, and I drove past, then I prayed, quietly and without jubilation.

This is the day that the Lord has made; let us rejoice and be glad in it.

* * *

Five in the morning is indeed a good time for prayer. The natural and human worlds emerge out of the dark and quiet into light and sound, and this encourages some sort of response, even if it is only to pause, wherever you are: Stop moving and doing and thinking, and just . . . behold.

BLESSING

Blessed is the spot
And the house
And the temple
And the city street
And the human heart
And the clinic
And the sidewalk
And the bridge
And the riverbank
And the refuge
And the stony beach
And the flowering orchard
And the cliff top
And the ice floe
And the barley field
And the deep woods
Blessed is the place
Where mention of God has been made
Where God's love has been offered and received
By human voices, by human ears, by blessed human hands.
Amen.
    KB

One of my favorite (optional) elements in a wedding is when I, as officiator, ask for a moment of silent prayer. This is more often done at outdoor weddings, particularly when the bride and groom are outdoorsy sorts of people—game wardens, for example. They anticipate that human silence will allow the voice of nature to be heard. And they are right: Nature promptly offers the fussy chirping of a songbird, the whine of an insect, or the lunatic giggle of a loon. These, with soft susurrations of wind and water, reliably join in some semblance of harmony. Given silence, moreover, both babies and stomachs take the opportunity to gurgle and faraway dogs to bark, while it is virtually guaranteed that an ambulance will pass at that moment, siren wailing, down the nearest roadway.

Why not? Stomachs, babies, dogs, and ambulances have their own valuable commentary to offer on the matrimonial condition. "True quiet is normally and quite naturally rare," I tell my friend, the one who longs for a quiet moment.

The modern world is noisy. Even in places that were once reliably dull—the bank, the post office, the departure lounge in an airport—the hush has been jazzed up with music, television screens, or (in the case of the airport) both.

Any passenger spends a minimum of an hour awaiting the departure of her flight, and this would seem an excellent time for unimpeded, prayerful contemplation. After all, she is about to be packed into intimate proximity to a hundred or more total strangers, any one of which might have halitosis, influenza, or explosives in his underpants. With a cargo of flesh and jet fuel, she will be flung into absurdly overcrowded skies thirty thousand feet above the earth, and only the attentive competence of the flight crew and some overworked traffic controllers stands between her and death.

Faced squarely, this is the sort of thing that can promote serious and earnest (even frantic) conversations with God. But maybe that's exactly what all the music and blathering screens are intended to forestall.

On the other hand, what hideous gorge of fear could possibly demand suppression when all we're doing is standing in line at the bank? I stayed in a hotel recently that had little movie screens mounted in the elevators, as though a compassionate hospitality professional wished to spare me seventeen seconds of excruciating boredom—the time it took to get from the lobby to the fifteenth floor. Here again, though, maybe it's fear rather than boredom that is the problem, since I probably will spend at least ten of those seventeen seconds wondering whether elevator cables ever actually snap, and if it's true that you can avoid death by jumping upward just at the moment of impact.

For those who dwell in the modern, industrialized West, the time we spend either asleep or dead is the only time in which we are expected to entertain ourselves; the bedroom, the one place—other than the grave—in which we can reasonably anticipate a diminution in an otherwise relentless barrage of sight and sound.

Associations between sleep and death are many and varied. One of the most urgent and obvious, at least from the point of view of our immediate ancestors, was that the former could so easily slide into the latter.

In old Maine graveyards, small gravestones offer mute testimony to what was once a heartbreakingly common phenomenon. *We have loved thee on earth, may we meet thee in heaven,* the gravestones say, beneath dates of birth and death that are only a few years or even mere months apart. Russian mothers used to press an icon of the Holy Mother against an ill child's chest, as if the Virgin might ease that labored breathing.

One of my classmates at seminary snorted contemptuously at this notion, which he termed irrational superstition. But my daughter Ellie has had pneumonia. I think of all the mothers across the centuries who had to sit beside their children, watching them struggle to take in air, and I can easily imagine trying anything—an icon, a penance, a lock of Elvis Presley's hair—that might (please? please?) let my Ellie live. Since we live in the developed world in the twenty-first century, Ellie received, instead of icons, the miracles of bottled oxygen, antibiotics, steroids, and an intensive care unit. *Thank you. Thank you. Thank you.*

Now I lay me down to sleep
I pray the Lord my soul to keep

If I should die before I wake
I pray the Lord my soul to take.

Bedtime prayers have their origins in the ubiquity of sudden, inexplicable loss. In the eighteenth and nineteenth centuries, pneumonia was the commonest way for death to arrive in the night hours, carrying off adults as well as children.

The child we tuck into bed tonight is almost certain to arise, hale, hearty, and demanding, tomorrow morning. If children in the old days were familiar enough with death to be able to say "If I should die before I wake" with stoic realism, our children today might be freaked out by that part, and if they aren't freaked out, their parents will be. That is, in itself, an indication of what we have to be thankful for.

Now I lay me down to sleep
I pray that love my soul will keep
My body rest, my love expand
To every soul in every land.
God bless . . .
Amen.

We are a diurnal species, heavily dependent on our vision for protection from predators. Darkness makes us vulnerable even before the unconsciousness of sleep suspends the rest of our defenses.

Children's prayers naturally include a request for safekeeping (*Through the darkness please be near me. Keep me safe till morning light*), but adult prayers admit vulnerability, too. A Samburu Kenyan prayer asks:

God save us
God hide us.
When we sleep, God, do not sleep
If we sleep, God, do not get drowsy,
Tie us around Your arm, God,
Like a bracelet.

While an old Celtic prayer says:

Lord and God of power,
Shield and sustain me this night.
Lord, God of power
This night and every night.

In its microcosmic foreshadowing of death and rebirth, in its offerings of the strange alternate reality of dreams, sleep has fascinated shamans, theologians, and later, psychologists, but sleep also recommends itself as a study subject for the evolutionary biologist. After all, eons of painstaking natural selection have bred in us the various means by which we might recognize and then defend ourselves from threats: In evolutionary terms, wouldn't an individual who did not sleep survive longer and therefore be apt to leave more surviving offspring than his somnolent competitors?

Unfortunately, no. Sleep deprivation is so painful and debilitating that interrogators have found it an effective means of torture. It can prove fatal if kept up long enough; a lack of sleep will kill you faster than a lack of food.

We generally think of sleep as a condition of dormancy, during which the body, relieved of the obligation to move and work, can repair itself and recoup energy. As it turns out, sleep is a surprisingly active state. While our limbs might enjoy a period of relative inactivity (remember that even normal sleep involves considerable twitching and thrashing), our cardiovascular, respiratory, digestive, and immune systems keep right on working. Meanwhile, however unconscious and thus unappreciative we may be of the fact, the brain remains capable of producing complex activities such as speech and walking (though the sleepwalker will tend to walk into walls). Even if we stay in bed with our mouths shut, our brains will fire away energetically all night long. Sleep isn't just resting, it's complex, dangerous, and therefore biologically expensive.

*　　*　　*

Like food, sleep—or, more precisely, dreams—features prominently in religious literature. Jacob, soon to be the progenitor of a great nation, dreams of a ladder reaching to the heavens, and his son Joseph (of coat-of-many-colors fame) becomes a professional dream interpreter, accurately predicting flood and famine from the dreams of his patron, Pharaoh. Through dreams, Pharaoh is warned of impending disaster should he fail to let Moses' people go. The Angel of the Lord comes to Joseph, Mary's fiancé, in a dream, to persuade him not to reject her just because she's pregnant.

It's not only the Jewish or Christian God who is so communicative through dreams: Alexander the Great, in the middle of his war against the Tyrians, dreamed that a satyr was dancing on his shield. You could interpret this any number of ways, but apparently, Alexander was told that he had dreamed a rebus. He may have seen pictures, but the dream's meaning was in the sound of the words. Since the word "satyr" sounds sort of like *sa tyros* (meaning roughly "Tyre is yours"), the dream clearly (if conveniently) predicted Alexander's triumph.

In ancient China, meanwhile, they were already considering what dreams have to say about the nature of reality: "There was a man who dreamed he was a butterfly," says the sage's story. "The butterfly flew joyfully among the flowers. Then the man awoke and was himself again. Now, did the man dream that he was a butterfly, or was there a butterfly somewhere dreaming it was a man?"

An evolutionary biologist would point out that insects, like reptiles, may have periods of dormancy, but they don't display the neural markers of true dreaming sleep. Mammals dream—think of your dog "chasing rabbits" in her sleep—and so do some birds. The human brain dreams according to a predictable pattern all night long. When, after a few preliminary phases, we switch into REM (or rapid eye movement) sleep, our hearts speed up, our blood pressure rises, we breathe more rapidly and irregularly, our eyes jump around, and the muscles in our arms and legs become temporarily paralyzed. (Oh—and men get woodies.) If someone wakes you up during REM sleep, you will remember dreaming.

Otherwise, we forget nearly all of our dreams. There is no such thing as deep, dreamless sleep, only sleep that is deep enough that we don't awaken from it during the night.

The notion that dreaming is important because dreams contain messages from God, fairies, or our own labyrinthine subconscious is appealing, but it doesn't seem to be why sleep is vital to our mental and physical health. Sleep deprivation will induce hallucinations that occur in patterns approximating a normal dreaming cycle, as if the brain, in its exhaustion, still struggles desperately to dream.

Biologist Francis Crick, among others, has focused his research on dreaming as a necessary neurological accompaniment to conscious experience. What Shakespeare described as "knitting up the raveled sleeve of care," Crick's model describes more prosaically as being akin to a computer's "defrag" program. The chaotic welter of sense impressions and experiences taken in during the conscious day are organized, sorted, and stored as learned information and memory throughout the unconscious night. Our dreams are the ancillary discharges of a brain busily tidying up the hard drive.

Consciousness is hard to define precisely, but it is generally described as the awareness of awareness; a self's recognition of itself and its own experience. Not coincidentally, consciousness can also be defined as *wakefulness*, and—interestingly—the phrase "she is unconscious" can describe a medical problem or a spiritual one.

Whatever consciousness is, snakes seem to get along well enough without it. If sleep exists so that we can dream, and dreams exist because of consciousness, what is so valuable to us (in Darwinian terms) about consciousness that it is worth the daily price of eight virtually defenseless hours of slumber?

Psychologist Nicholas Humphrey proposes that consciousness enhances what is called the "assimilation tendency": the tendency that human beings and other conscious creatures have to communicate. People talk to their dogs, and dogs wag their tails at human beings. This could be (indeed, has been) interpreted as a foolish error in human and beast, but it's worth noting that both the dog and the human are able to understand each other. Moreover, a dog can correctly interpret the anger signals of a horse, even if the dog doesn't have hooves to stamp or a mane to shake.

Having an awareness of its own subjective mental state would increase an animal's ability to interpret the mental state of other animals by allowing it to draw a kind of analogy to their experience. This ability would have obvious benefits for any social animal—if you are a subordinate baboon, it really is helpful to be able to tell when the dominant male is in a rotten mood, especially given the male baboon's enormous, sharp teeth. Meanwhile, a wolf might use this talent to more accurately assess a deer's vigorous fine fettle or fatigue, while the deer might interpret the behavior of a discouraged wolf and conclude that freaking out and wasting valuable energy reserves by running away isn't worth it.

Can animals really look at another animal belonging to a different species, interpret its particular, species-specific signals, and accurately assess its mood? Ask your dog—and you can use words. She'll answer you.

This awareness of another's state of mind is called empathy. An empathetic creature can "feel into" the experience of another— that's what the word literally means. According to Professors Salk and Humphrey, we are conscious so that we may be empathetic, and the more fully conscious we become, the more we will be able to empathize with those around us.

Does this, by any chance, sound familiar?

The goal of spiritual practice is to increase conscious awareness. "Wake up!" is the challenge we hear from the Buddha, from Jesus, from the Sufi master, from the Hindu yogi, from the psalmist who sings:

Awake, my soul!
Awake, O harp and lyre!
I will awake the dawn.
Psalm 108

Jesus and the first-century Essene rabbi Hillel responded to a similar question with an identical answer: What is the greatest of the Commandments?

"First . . . you shall love the Lord your God with all your heart, and with all your soul, and with all your mind, and with all your strength. The second is this, You shall love your neighbor as yourself."

All else, as Hillel said, is commentary.

The Truth—that there is a reciprocal link between consciousness and empathy—that has been insisted upon for centuries by the great spiritual teachers and mystics worldwide might just turn out to be a scientific truth, too. Wouldn't that be cool?

Though it has become considerably safer, sleep remains mysterious and even a little frightening. "At night, prisoners forget their prison . . . at night governors forget their power," writes the Sufi poet Rumi. Self-forgetting is what we welcome and what we fear in sleep.

In dreams we fly, and flight is glorious, or we plummet downward, howling, and awaken suddenly, hearts pounding, struggling to remember where and who we are: governor or prisoner? Sage or butterfly? Because we don't know what the night will bring, because we will not necessarily remember what the night has held, bedtime is, as it has always been, a time that lends itself to prayer. Knowing of the connection between sleep and consciousness, dreams and empathy, I prefer my nighttime prayers to acknowledge fear but emphasize compassion.

Watch, dear Lord, with those who wake
Or watch, or work or weep tonight,
And give your angels charge
Over those who sleep.
Tend your sick ones, O Lord God
Rest your weary ones.
Bless your dying ones.

Soothe your suffering ones.
Pity your afflicted ones.
Shield your joyous ones.
All for your love's sake.
Amen.

      St. Augustine

In *A Child's Good Night Book*, author Margaret Wise Brown offers a couple of lovely lines that sound very much like a traditional bedtime prayer. "Dear Father, hear and bless thy beasts and singing birds, and guard with tenderness small things that have no words," has served me nicely as a graveside prayer for a departed hamster as well as when called upon at short notice to preside over the roadside death of a moose.

ADULT'S BEDTIME PRAYER

O God, I offer the prayers of my heart.
May I be held in your hands as I sleep.
May I be blessed by your love. May I arise with joy in the
    morning.
For those I name aloud [names],
May they be held in your hands and blessed by your love.
May they arise with joy in the morning.
For those whose names I do not know but whose sufferings I
    know to be real to you,
Help me, that they might become real to me.
May they be held in your hands and blessed by your love.
May they arise with joy in the morning.
Amen.

    KB

5

Lovers' Prayers

"That's not what I'd call an adult's bedtime prayer," said game warden Jesse Gillespie when I showed him what I had written about prayer and sleep. He said it with a grin, though whether by that grin he hoped to emphasize or disavow the innuendo wasn't clear to me.

And so: "Are you talking about sex?" his chaplain asked him, and he blushed.

Gillespie had just gotten back together with his wife. He was a little, shall we say, ebullient? I'll have to forgive him.

Or is there anything to forgive?

As this young man was forced to admit, the word "bedtime" brings activities to mind that don't necessarily accord with ordinary notions of appropriate spiritual observance. Gillespie confessed that when he was an adolescent being brought up Presbyterian, turning his thoughts to God was a surefire way to deal with unwanted boners.

As an adult man joyfully reacquainting himself with the delights of marital canoodling, and using a language in which "going to bed" or "sleeping with" is a euphemism for sex, Gillespie dismissed bedtime prayers as unapplicable to his real life. "And you are supposed to be writing about real life," he pointed out. "Aren't you?"

May these vows and this marriage be blessed.
May this marriage be delicious milk,
Like wine and halvah.
May it offer fruit and shade
Like the date palm.
May this marriage be full of laughter
Making every day a day in Paradise
May this marriage be a token of compassion
A seal of joy now and forever more.
May this marriage have a gracious face and a good name,
An omen as welcome
As the moon in a clear, daylight sky.
I have run out of words to describe
How spirit mingles in this marriage!
        Jalil al-Din Rumi

("Well, okay," says Gillespie. "But that guy wasn't a Presbyterian, was he?")

Imagine a bored thirteen-year-old, prematurely jaded after the fashion of our era, picking up a Christian Bible for the first time. The Bible falls open at this passage from the Hebrew Scriptures (aka the Old Testament).

How fair and pleasant you are
O loved one, delectable maiden
You are stately as a palm tree
And your breasts are its clusters

"Dang!" says the thirteen-year-old. "This is the Bible?"

I say I will climb the palm tree
And lay hold of its branches
Oh may your breasts be like clusters of the vine
And the scent of your breath like apples

Your kisses like the best wine
That goes down smoothly
Gliding over lips and teeth . . .

And another biblical scholar is born.

"Gillespie," I say. "I'm going to write you a prescription."

I mark a page and press my small pocket Bible into his reluctant hands.

Oh may your breasts be like clusters of the vine . . . It is the Song of Solomon, a slim volume sandwiched between the pessimism of Ecclesiastes and the raging eloquence of Isaiah.

Ecclesiastes offers its dour remarks about life's ultimate limitations. Isaiah delivers tirades about the Divine disappointment with an iniquitous people. In between there is this strange, incandescent erotic poem. What in heaven's name is it doing in the Bible?

The traditional explanation for this apparent anomaly is that the poem was never intended for a flesh-and-blood lover but is instead an allegorical paean to God. This can be difficult to wrap your mind around, and when you return to the text, it is even more difficult to keep your mind thus wrapped:

How graceful are your feet in sandals,
O queenly maiden!
Your rounded thighs are like jewels
the work of a master hand.
Your navel is a rounded bowl
that never lacks mixed wine.
Your belly is a heap of wheat,
encircled with lilies . . .

"Dang!" says Gillespie, and takes the Bible home to show his wife.

I was at lunch with several minister friends one day when I happened to mention that, having been invited to preach for a local congregation, I thought I would offer a sermon on the Song of Solomon. The reaction was uniform: "Are you out of your mind?"

"I never preach on that book, Sister Kate," my Baptist friend Moira confessed. "I don't even mention the name of it out loud unless I'm sure the members of the youth group are out of earshot."

Moira wasn't alone. According to my admittedly informal poll of clergy colleagues, your average preacher is far more comfortable reading aloud those passages from Isaiah in which God claims His people are wallowing in their ignorance and vice "like a drunkard in his own vomit" than he is standing in the pulpit holding forth about God's breasts and God's thighs, the milk and honey that may be tasted beneath God's tongue.

I wonder if the youth group at Moira's church is allowed to read the biblical stories in which Herod slaughters all the little boy babies after hearing of the birth of baby Jesus, or the one in which innocent Tamar is raped. A question for another day. Let it simply be acknowledged that the Song of Solomon is one of the most unjustly neglected books in the Bible. Neither those who embrace the Bible nor those who reject it seem to remember that the book is there at all.

Ram Dass began life as a nice Jewish boy who grew into a nice Hindu man. He has been interpreting and explaining Hinduism for Western audiences since the 1970s and is perhaps best known for his classic, *Be Here Now.*

In the Hindu tradition, Ram Dass tells us, God assumes many forms and takes on many roles. The most astonishing one, for Westerners, is probably that of the god Krishna.

In a famous story about Krishna, the god is about seventeen years old and unbelievably good-looking. Nice white teeth, pretty eyes, cute tush, and he's talented, too. He plays his flute so beautifully that thousands of women leave their husbands, babies, and pots cooking on the stove to go to him. Milkmaids jump up from their milking stools and cast aside their milk pails, and all these women rush to be with Krishna. So Krishna manifests himself in thousands of forms, one for each woman, and makes love to each of them just as she would most like to be made love to.

Which sounds like something parental controls are supposed to keep off the screens of immature Web surfers, but the thing is, the milkmaids in the story are *making love to God*. It's fun, presumably, but it's also religious. (Imagine! Fun and religious! What a concept!) In India, the story of Krishna and the milkmaids is commemorated by a holiday that is celebrated pretty much the way Passover or Easter is celebrated in the West.

There is also a sect of Krishna worshippers in India known as the Gopis, who are all men. They aren't transvestites, but part of their ritual is to dress up as the milkmaids in the story. There are lots of ways for a Hindu to ritually express the relationship of devotee to Divine: You can be parent to child, child to parent, friend to friend. In the Gopis' case, worship takes the form of being in relation to the god Krishna as lover to lover.

Jehovah has a very limited repertoire of emotional responses, Ram Dass has said: "He can be righteous, he can be indignant, he can be punitive, he can be benevolent. But that's about it."

Ah! But Ram Dass has forgotten about the Song of Solomon. Right smack dab in the middle of that stern and rigid, grumping-Jehovah portion of the Hebrew scripture, readers find themselves called to worship God just like Gopis: lover to lover.

Now, wait just a minute, you may be saying. Did the author of the Song of Solomon really intend for the poem to be read as if God were the object of its voluptuous affection?

Well. If we want to be extremely sensible and rational, we can agree that this was probably poetry originally written by and for human lovers, like Shakespeare's sonnets, or Elizabeth Barrett Browning's "How do I love thee? Let me count the ways," though, frankly, a lot sexier.

The Bible is an anthology, a collection of diverse texts from different times written in many different genres. Some are clearly intended to be religious in our ordinary sense of the word, while others are what we would think of as secular. There are poems, prayers and song lyrics, fables, letters, histories, and quite detailed instructions for building arks and temples.

Our ancestors did not divide the secular and the sacred with quite the same firmness that we do. History could be sacred, laws could be sacred, prayers, fables, and aphorisms were sacred, and by the evidence of its inclusion in scripture, erotic love poetry could be considered sacred, too.

Why not? How hard is it to imagine Elizabeth Barrett Browning addressing her question to God? Couldn't you sing a hymn that sounded like this: God loves you, *yeah, yeah, yeah! With a love like that, you know you should be glad.*

Here is a brief (very brief, I promise) foray into biblical criticism: There are two theological intentions you should consider in assessing any biblical text. The first is the theological intention of the author. The other, and perhaps the more important one, is the theological intention of the *editor.*

We don't know what the author had in mind while writing the Song of Solomon—well, let me rephrase that. We know exactly what he or she had in mind:

O . . . wind!
Blow upon my garden
that its fragrance may be wafted abroad.
Let my beloved come to his garden,
and eat its choicest fruits.

What we can't know is *whom* he or she had in mind. But we can make some reasonable assumptions about whom the redactor or editor had in mind when he or she included this among the most sacred scripture of his or her people. And we know Whom we have in mind when—or if—we are brave enough to read these words aloud within the sanctuary of our church.

Set me as a seal upon your heart,
as a seal upon your arm;

for love is strong as death,
passion fierce as the grave.
Its flashes are flashes of fire . . .

God is love, the Bible says, but when it comes to sexual pair bonds and the families produced thereby, love is not a given. Misery and evil are distinct possibilities. Within a single generation of the Fall, after all, we have the story of Cain and Abel and the first of the fratricides, oppressions, rapes, and moral failures chronicled with such depressing regularity in the Bible.

God has evidently created a species in dire need of redemption. It is a species only love and creativity might redeem.

God has also created a species some of whose members, in turn, created a Book that only love and creativity can redeem. God is re-created in loving creativity and procreativity, and what is a love poem if not creativity and procreativity? So what finer, more enjoyable redemption might there be than this?

As an apple tree among the trees of the wood,
so is my beloved among young men.
With great delight I sat in his shadow,
and his fruit was sweet to my taste.
He brought me to the banqueting house,
and his intention toward me was love . . .

The cognitive dissonance that arises out of reading the Song of Solomon as scripture makes theologians and pastors perspire. Perhaps some of my readers are unconvinced as well.

Perhaps you have been officially pair-bonded, married (or the closest possible alternative thereto), for quite some time. You've had a chance to settle in a bit and are no longer as inclined to such paroxysms of ebullient, embarrassing poetic feeling as you might have been once. Perhaps you are flawed and a finder of flaws, and because of this, you've come to think love is damned hard. Well, true love, real, lasting, committed love between two human beings (imperfect and at least sometimes unlovable by definition), *is* hard.

It's impossible.

Or it would be if not for the fact that with God, all things are possible. If we learn to see as if with the eyes of God, and to give as if from the heart of God, then we might be able to get a glimpse of who the Beloved truly is.

In such a glimpse, the merely human is transfigured before our eyes, face shining like the sun. In such a moment, a wild, illogical, absurd romance is encircled by and defined as the word of God. And we are speaking it.

My beloved is mine and I am his . . .

"Arise, my love, my fair one, and come away . . ."

6

Pausing on the Threshold for Prayer

May the road rise to meet you,
May the wind be always at your back
May the rains fall soft upon your fields
And until we meet again
May God hold you in the palm of His hand.
     Irish Blessing

We didn't have television when my children were younger, but they did get to watch a movie on the weekends and so discovered early the virtues of a remote-control pause button. If, in the middle of *The Lion King*, someone had to pee, he or she would shout "Pause!" and whoever had charge of the remote was honor-bound to press the button.

The word, and the idea, leaked into their play. A child might shout "Pause" to stop a game of tag for a drink of water or "Pause" to interrupt a sibling's story long enough to point out inconsistencies in the plot. It was an imperative issued and obeyed as absolutely as "Dibs" or "Jinx-Pinx! You owe me a Coke."

Once I was remonstrating with my son Peter about something, and he actually held out his hand, palm up, thumb bent, as if reaching around a remote control to press a button. "Pause!" he shouted, and I was so astonished, I stopped speaking. This gave him time to explain that it was his sister, not he, who had committed the crime du jour: spilling the compost bucket in the middle of the backyard, neglecting to feed the dog, or sending a Tonka truck filled with confectioners' sugar down the stairs to make a satisfactorily smoky "hazmat accident" in the front hall.

Grace, prayer, or blessing: These are moments to pause and make room in life for clarity, attention, and gratitude. The problem is that a lamentably inattentive person like me needs some sort of external reminder when it comes to spiritual practice, and my community doesn't offer the traditional ones. No muezzin ascends his tower to send a call to prayer echoing over the gently smoking chimneys of my Maine community. Nor do great bells peal or even tinkle.

Thich Nhat Hanh talks about finding "bells of mindfulness" in daily life—phenomena that you are likely to encounter that can trigger a moment of conscious attention, such as a ringing telephone or the brake lights of the car in front of you, which Thay, or teacher, as he is called, sees as the eyes of Buddha, signaling you to be aware. As bells of mindfulness go, meals and bedtime work well, and other ordinary elements of our modern lives are similarly useful in their regularity, predictability, and intrinsic significance.

You can say a threshold blessing with, to, or about any member of the household as he or she departs from home, whether it is to go to school, to work, or to Bermuda. Such a pause recognizes the crossing of a boundary between interior and exterior, known and unknown, self and other, parent and child, and potentially at least, life and death.

My friend Tom Ballard is a state trooper. He was in my husband, Drew's, graduating class at the Maine Criminal Justice Academy, and the family friendship that began there continued up to and beyond Drew's death in 1996. Tom and his wife, Tonya, have two children, Michael and Meghan, who are now adults, but they were little—ten and five, respectively—when their "uncle" Drew died.

fish. Being offered a small snack partway through the service was a humane gesture, I thought, given all the confusing standing up, sitting down, and kneeling that Catholicism otherwise appeared to consist of.

Mr. Belfiore took these things seriously, however. He had considered entering the priesthood before he met Natasha's mother and was more religious than anyone I'd ever met.

Because I spent a lot of time at the Belfiores', the blessing Mr. Belfiore offered his children whenever they left the house was planted in my memory as well as theirs. Even when Natasha and I were thirteen and intent on some adolescent adventure, he always made us pause for his prayer, brushing aside our protests. "Da-ad, the movie starts in fifteen minutes. Come on, Dad, d'you really have to . . ."

Mr. Belfiore would calmly take his daughter's face between his hands, gaze adoringly at her with the warm brown eyes she had inherited from him, and say:

May the Lord bless and keep you
May the Lord make His face to shine upon you and be gracious
    unto you
May the Lord lift up His countenance upon you
And give you peace.

We didn't do anything like this in my family. If we had, I suppose I might have taken it for granted or—because I would have attached to this paternal gesture all the tensions and conflicts seething within me—resented it. I'm sure I would have argued with my father's purposes and at some point rejected both his worthiness and his capacity to speak to me of God.

As it was, dancing impatiently on the linoleum in the Belfiores' kitchen, my hand on the knob of their back door, I watched Natasha roll her eyes and submit to this exotic ritual: a father's blessing. I was envious.

Like my mother, I spent my twenties keeping the home fires burning and looking after small children. When my youngest was born, my eldest was six (yes, I know: We weren't so good at birth control). I did not have a household staff. So getting everybody up, dressed, fed, and over the threshold in the morning was a major operation.

Assuming everyone who needed one had a clean diaper, and assuming the diapers stayed clean for at least twenty minutes, there were then eight small socks to find (few clean, none matching), at least one bulbous head to rescue from the neckline of a sweater I'd forgotten to unbutton, eccentricities to accommodate (Ellie put her overalls on backward, Zach claimed striped socks hurt his feet), and then all those snow pants and jackets to zip and snap, little thumbs to prod into the right place in eight little mittens, assuming I could find eight mittens and didn't have to substitute a sock ("Okay, Zach, *not* a striped sock"), and snow boots that still fit and weren't wet inside. Assuming—and these are assumptions— everyone then made it out the door before someone announced that he or she needed to pee (or just had), everyone still had to be loaded into car seats crunchy with rice cake crumbs (source of discomfort or serendipitous snack? it depended on the kid). I'd start the car with a sock over my hand, because the steering wheel was cold and I was the one who got stuck without a mitten.

One winter morning, late (as usual), I set off with the kids to drive Zach to first grade. We'd driven all the way through town and were about five miles from home when I happened to glance back over my shoulder. The baby's car seat was empty.

I forgot the baby.

Hands trembling, I turned the car around and drove home with extravagant care, lest we all get into a horrible accident, praying the all-purpose emergency prayer (*OhGodOhGodOhGod*), with minor variations:

Please please please don't let anything bad happen to Woolie . . .
O God, I'm a terrible mother.
O God, I shouldn't have had four children.
Etc.

Bursting through the back door, I found Woolie lying on a blanket where I'd left her in the middle of the kitchen floor. She was sucking her fingers and kicking her legs. The dog sat beside her, regarding her with a puzzled expression (*usually they take all their puppies with them*).

Oh God. Thank God. Thank God. Thank God.

If I had to do it over again, I would emulate Michael, Meghan, and Mr. Belfiore: I would make a threshold prayer part of the family routine right from the start. (Who knows? If I had paused to offer a blessing to my children before we left the house that morning, I might have noticed one was missing.)

It probably wouldn't have been the prayer Natasha's dad used to say to her, drawing his thumb across her forehead to make a tender cross: "May the Lord bless and keep you . . ."

That would have sounded way too religious for me then. It definitely sounded too religious for Natasha, who found the Catholic obligations of her childhood onerous. Still, though she is no longer a practicing Catholic or any kind of religious, Natasha admits that her father's threshold blessing felt like love and was love.

Incidentally, I can't claim to have been the rare and saintly person possessed of the endless patience, tolerance, and attention to detail that motherhood demands. Motherhood could demand until it was blue in the face. I was an impatient, disorganized, restless, and resentful mother at least half the time. When my advice is solicited, I recommend against having four children in six years: It's a lot of hard, boring work, and the intense emotional connection I felt to my children too often prompted me to feel overwhelmed and guilty rather than affectionate and maternal. A threshold prayer would have "worked" the way the mealtime grace and the bedtime prayers do: by allowing reality to rise and be acknowledged. I don't mean the reality of the backward overalls, the irritation, and the striped socks. I mean the real reality, the truth about who each of us was and what it meant to be living our lives together.

* * *

This is how I most often bless my children, even though I didn't start to do it until they were taller than I am, so I have to crane my neck back and peer upward to meet their gaze:

> May love and strength be in your hands
> May love and courage be in your heart
> May love and wisdom be in your mind
> May God go with you and work through you
> Today and in all your days.
> Amen.
>
> KB

It's a very simple blessing, easy to do with children but not too babyish for an adult to receive. Hand motions go along with the words, and you can do these instead of the words if hearing impairments, a noisy environment, or a sore throat precludes spoken prayers.

"May love and strength be in your hands," you'll say, and hold your hands out, palms up. "May love and courage be in your heart," and your hands rest, one atop the other, against your chest. "May love and wisdom be in your mind," and your palms press against your forehead before you raise them in the air and say the last line: "May God be with you and work through you, today and in all your days."

I taught Ruth this prayer in the hospital in the middle of the night that Nina was born. Touch the baby's hands . . . touch the baby's heart . . . touch the baby's forehead . . . hold your palms over the baby: "today and in all your days, oh, you perfect little cupcake, you yummy little schnoogums," etc.

Perhaps now is a good time to mention that this prayer, like all the prayers I use or recommend, can be adapted and not just by middle-aged ministers who lose all sense and dignity at the sight of a sweet little baby.

I'll explain why a person might want or need to adapt a prayer in Chapters 15 and 16, but suffice to say that the word "God" can be replaced with "Christ," "love," "peace," or—for *Star Wars* fans—"The Force."

Prayers are not recipes or formulae, they are love poems. They need not be factual, but they must be true.

> May all I say
> And all I do
> Be in harmony with thee
> God within me
> God beyond me
> Maker of the trees.
>
> Iroquois Prayer

There are plenty of other prayers that suit the moment on the threshold, even if ain't nobody here can cross it for you and you gotta cross it by yourself.

> Day by day, dear Lord,
> These things I pray . . .
> To see Thee more clearly,
> Love Thee more dearly,
> And to follow Thee more nearly,
> Day by day.

The words of the prayer are attributed to Richard of Chichester and adapted by John Farnham. Because I first heard it as a groovy sixties-era flower-child anthem from the musical *Godspell,* the tune inevitably begins to play in my head along with images of long-haired Jesus freaks with tie-dyed dashikis and dazed smiles. Still, if allowances are made for the epiphenomena, it's really a damned good prayer. Like the Serenity Prayer: once you've said it, you've said everything that needs saying. Stop praying and get going.

One more threshold blessing for the truly time-challenged:
Vaya con Dios! (Go with God!)

PART TWO

Siren Calls

7

In Praise of a Little Hypocrisy

Now when the Pharisees and some of the scribes who had come from Jerusalem gathered around [Jesus], they noticed that some of his disciples were eating with defiled hands, that is, without washing them. (For the Pharisees, and all the Jews, do not eat unless they thoroughly wash their hands, thus observing the traditions of their elders; and they do not eat anything from the market unless they wash it; and there are also many other traditions they observe, such as the washing of cups, pots, and bronze kettles.) So the Pharisees and the scribes asked him, "Why do your disciples not live according to the tradition of the elders, but eat with defiled hands?" He said to them, "Isaiah prophesied rightly about you hypocrites, as it is written, 'This people honors me with their lips, but their hearts are far from me; in vain do they worship me, teaching human precepts as doctrines.' You abandon the commandment of God and hold to human tradition."

Mark 7

For several years, I had a total of six teenagers around the house. Like Jesus, like the prophets of old, they frequently took it upon themselves to name moments wherein my claim to honor the Commandments of God or, more to the point, to make *them* honor the Commandments of God, had been contradicted by my behavior. Perhaps it was because I was surrounded by so many self-anointed prophets that I began to think more kindly of hypocrisy.

While I was a student minister for a Unitarian Universalist church in Pittsfield, Maine, I had to come up with a sermon theme every week, so I was always pleased when one fell serendipitously into my lap, especially on a Monday morning. One particular Monday, one of my children—I can't remember which one—had forgotten all about a school homework assignment that required bringing in a quote from a notable woman. The child found this one at the back of my battered Unitarian Universalist hymnal:

> Never doubt that a small group of committed, thoughtful people can change the world. Indeed, it is the only thing that ever has.
>
> Margaret Mead

"Eureka!" the child shouted.

"Eureka!" I echoed, and dashed to my desk. *Never Doubt,* I typed at the top of my computer screen, and pressed save, thinking that when I actually sat down to write the sermon, the end result would inspire a small group of thoughtful, committed citizens—the Unitarian Universalists of Pittsfield—to change the world. With wars in Iraq and Afghanistan, and the catastrophe in New Orleans making headlines, the world seemed much in need of changing.

As the week went on, however, I found myself bothered by that quote.

Never doubt that a small group of committed, thoughtful people can change the world, but Unitarian Universalism is the religion of the dubious. We *like* doubt. Even if we think of ourselves as drawing on the wisdom of all the world's religions, we proudly doubt and deny the exclusive claim to truth that any one of these would make.

A Unitarian Universalist Christian, for example, is a Christian willing to share a pew with one or more non-Christians who,

the Unitarian Universalists of Pittsfield, Maine—is invited to think of itself as those thoughtful, committed citizens, the ones who are going to change the world.

I don't know if the members of a small church in rural Maine could change the world. In any event, we are unlikely to change it as suddenly and dramatically as the September 11 hijackers, if only because even the most fundamentalist among us would be unlikely to find authorization for bombing buildings on our list of principles and purposes, or in the Constitution of the United States of America.

As modern, post-Enlightenment, religiously diverse Americans, we are constantly challenged to make a clear-eyed examination of both political and religious authority. As enfranchised citizens, we are called to look for the gaps between word and behavior, between what is claimed and what is lived—by ourselves, incidentally, as well as by the likes of Jerry Falwell, Jeremiah Wright, George Bush, or Barack Obama. Which is to say we are called to look for hope.

The prophet can be defined as a proud doubter, looking askance at the talking, walking faithful, naming as merely human what can be no substitute for the Commandments of God. Love one another, the Commandment says.

"O my people!" cries the prophet. "Do you believe . . . or don't you?"

MORNING PRAYER,
ADAPTED FROM PSALM 51

"Create in me a clean heart, O God; and renew a right spirit
     within me."
Let the Light that can glow gently be a searchlight
Harsh and stubborn, for the Word is simple, but the way is hard
     and I am too inclined
To think
I have already reached the place to which I have been called by
     love,

And long to be.
"Open thou my lips; and my mouth shall show forth thy praise."
Before I can distract myself with other things, before I've charmed
	myself
With pleasures, comforts, the self-convincing clamor of my Self;
That idol
Who so easily wins the substance of my worship: Scour my heart
"The sacrifices of God are a broken spirit; a broken and a contrite
	heart."
I am too smart to break, too sure for contrition, too filled
With unimaginative theories that conveniently find You in Me,
	Your will
In my desires.
O blessed, jealous God, who will not suffer idols
My God, whose name is love and whose work is justice
Let the light that can glow softly be a beacon shining clear,
Let no sorrow reach my ears and find me indifferent
Let no human face come before me only to find me blind
"A broken and a contrite heart, O God, thou wilt not despise."
I am the instrument of thy labor: May your unrelenting love
Scour my heart and make me fit for thy use.
Amen.

8

Considering the Grace That Saves

O God, you know my folly
The wrongs I have done are not hidden from you.
Do not let those who hope in you
Be put to shame because of me,
O Lord God of hosts;
Do not let those who seek you be dishonored
Because of me.
Send out your light and your truth
Let them lead me
Let them bring me to your holy hill
And to your dwelling
Then I will go to the altar of God
To God my exceeding joy;
And I will praise you with the harp
O God, my God.

> Adapted from Psalms 69 and 43

"Father, into your hands I commend my spirit," Jesus said. And then he died.

Now, when the centurion who was keeping watch over Jesus saw the earthquake and its aftermath, he was terrified and said, "Certainly, this man was innocent." Or else he said: "Truly, this man was God's son!" Accounts vary, but maybe it is more or less the same thing. Jesus was God's son. He was also and therefore uniquely innocent.

Who was the centurion? The centurion was a Roman soldier.

My son Peter draws soldiers and elaborate battle scenes. Nowadays, the combatants are usually samurai, but when he was little, he took his inspiration from World War II. The military vehicles belonging to the good guys were drawn with little American flags flying from their antennae and prominent labels reading u.s.

The bad guys had swastikas on their tanks and labels, too.

The bad guys were the Nazis. He spelled it N-O-T-S-E-E-S. The Not-Sees. (It's so perfect, isn't it?)

So, which was the centurion? Was he one of the U.S., one of us? Or was he a Not-See? He was, we are told, the first gentile witness to the divinity of Christ.

Standing before the cross, he offered the first public utterance by a non-Jew of the Christian truth: *This man was innocent; this man is the son of God.*

The centurion was a commanding officer of a Roman army unit called a century, nominally a hundred foot soldiers. A centurion represented the most experienced and best informed of Caesar's soldiers in Roman-occupied Palestine. One of his responsibilities was the supervision of scourging and executions.

Therefore, the centurion standing at the foot of the cross, facing Christ, was not there by happenstance. It was his job to supervise the beating that Jesus had received, to see that he was correctly set upon the cross beside a public way so that all who passed could add to his agony by watching it.

The centurion had not condemned Jesus. He could neither condemn nor spare; his job was to oversee the execution. On his order, Jesus and the others were stripped and pressed down against the rough wood of the cross. On his word, the nails were driven into the wrists and feet of the robbers, into the wrists and feet of Christ. Doubtless the condemned cried out, but the centurion would not have flinched. He had to be sure that the nails were placed just so, not into the weak flesh but here and here, where the tendons run, strong as straps that can carry the weight of a man. As Jesus and the others were hoisted aloft, the centurion watched their suffering with an experienced eye. The crucified could last a long time on the cross. The centurion stood there.

Death was all around him. This was ordinary. It was the blamelessness of Christ that made his execution into murder. Death is all around our centurion when he looks up and sees Jesus, dead.

He makes his announcement into air that is filled with the moans of the dying, the weeping of mourners, the scent of blood. "Truly, this man was innocent, the Son of God," he says. And we are meant to be impressed by this? To count him one of us?

The centurion reminds me of the Walrus in Lewis Carroll's poem, the one who salts his meal of oysters with repentance and claims the right to weep for his victims even as they slide silkily down his throat.

Whether or not the centurion was a good guy, I'm pretty sure I'm one.

I'm a nice lady, a mother, and a law-enforcement chaplain. I saw the light—*Nothing matters more than love!*—and became an ordained servant of God. A little American flag flies from the antenna of my family van.

Just in case you need more evidence, though, here's a good thing I did:

There was a woman ahead of me in line one day at Shop 'n Save, and she had four small children. For obvious reasons, I tend to respond in certain ways to a quartet of little faces, so I made googly eyes at them while their mother carefully unloaded her shopping cart onto the conveyer belt.

"I gotta watch how much it ends up being," she said to the cashier. "Because I'm paying with a check from the food pantry."

Thinking of all the cans I lug to church for the cause, I said, "I didn't know that the food pantry can give out checks," and the woman answered yes, but the amount was limited, in her case to seventy-two dollars, and she wasn't sure but she feared she might go over the line. Then, of course, both the cashier and I began watching the lighted numbers tick past on the register display, even as the woman told us the story of how her life had fallen apart.

"He left without warning, my husband did, and didn't leave me no money. The rent is due. The landlady is patient, but no one is patient forever. So I've got this seventy-two-dollar check from the food pantry, but I really can't say what I am going to do about my life in the long run."

The cashier swept the last items across the scanner. A total flashed on the screen: seventy-six dollars and something-something cents. A sigh of disappointment from the woman, echoed by me, echoed by the cashier, echoed by the children.

"Well," the woman said in a heavy voice. "Well . . . shoot." She pawed through groceries heaped up at the far end of the conveyer belt and selected two items. She handed them to the cashier. "Guess I'll do without these. I'm sorry."

"That's all right," said the cashier kindly.

"Wait wait wait," I said. "Wait. Listen, give me those things. After they've been scanned with my stuff, I'll just hand them over to you and you can be on your way."

"Oh, no," said the woman. "You can't do that!"

"Of course I can."

"I couldn't let you—"

"I've got four children," I said. "I have been a single mother. I know how it goes."

The cashier held the packages in her hands, looking from me to the woman and back again, waiting. "But still . . ."

"It's not that big a deal. Please. Let me do this."

"All right," the woman said at last. The cashier placed the items—a box of Band-Aids and a package of baloney—on my side of the little plastic dividing rod. The woman and I and the cashier and the four children all looked at the box and the package, and then we looked at one another. Suddenly, we were all beaming like nitwits, as if we had just accomplished something marvelous! If it had been a movie, there would have been a burst of singing from a choir, a sudden wash of yellow light. We were . . . how else to describe this? We were all transfixed by the most ludicrous, lovely *joy*.

The moment passed. The cashier scanned the package of baloney, the box of Band-Aids, and handed them to the woman, who placed them in her plastic grocery sack. She said thank you to me again, several times, and I said, "You're welcome. Really. *De nada*. Thank you."

Later, driving home, my heart still light, I began to laugh. I realized, you see, that the two items I had purchased for this woman symbolized nicely just what one tends to get when one turns to a minister in time of need.

Baloney and Band-Aids.

Stranger still, it is often, by grace, enough.

But more about grace in a moment: Can we agree that I succeeded at love? That I did a good thing by purchasing the baloney and the Band-Aids for this woman?

Repeat after me: Kate did a good thing. Ready?

KATE DID A GOOD THING.

Ha! Take that, John Calvin! Don't I deserve to go to heaven, where the sun shines in perpetuity upon the just?

I have to make a confession, however. The reason I was paying attention to this woman's situation to begin with is that my Welfare Radar was on. For some unpleasant reason, I pay more attention to the food purchases of people who are paying for their groceries with public money than I do those who pay with their ATM card, like me. I was checking to see if she was buying groceries that I, the taxpayer, might approve of: dry beans and whole wheat bread.

So, okay, the original gaze I turned in her direction might not have been hostile, exactly, but it would be difficult to call it agapaic, charitable, brotherly, or even just kind.

How much *caritas* did the woman receive from me, anyway? In monetary terms, the box of Band-Aids and the package of baloney cost around four bucks. (Talk about cheap grace!) If her kids are anything like my own, neither the baloney nor the Band-Aids lasted longer than three days. Meanwhile, she was still without a husband, and the patience of the landlady was still slowly wearing thin. The Band-Aids and baloney I gave to her would not, could not, change her life.

Maybe her husband left because she cheated on him? And maybe she actually had four dollars in her pocket but was saving it for cigarettes or booze?

So I'm not perfect. Fine! Granted! But what imperfections might she have brought to this transaction?

There must have been some. There always are.

So there we were, giver and receiver, in all our limitation, in all our imperfection. The baloney and the Band-Aids passed from one side of the little plastic divider to the other, and for one precious moment, our shabby selves were joined, one to another, in wholeness. We were *in love*, all of us, the clerk and the kiddies, too, illumined in saffron while cherubim and seraphim, somewhere up in the rafters of the Rockland Shop 'n Save, began to sing.

Who was this guy, this centurion, to be a receiver of grace?

Jesus, innocent, dies.

In the unnatural darkness that had fallen, feeling the ground shake beneath him, hearing cries of terror echoing in the city as the veil of the temple rent itself in two like a woman tearing her hair in grief, the centurion glances up. And something *happens* to him.

"Truly, this man was innocent, the son of God," the centurion said, and praises God, and this is all we are told, as if this is somehow enough.

In what voice did he speak these first words of gentile witness? Did he pronounce them crisply, as a military command? Did he whisper them? Moan them? Or were they cried as if torn from the mouth of one whose heart had been pierced through by a vision too glorious, a love too perfect to bear?

My God, my God. Why have I forsaken you?

What do you say, and how do you say it, when it suddenly becomes clear to you that you have just murdered the Son of God?

* * *

Not too long after my first husband died, the kids and I headed south to Washington, D.C., to visit my family. I am a distracted driver at the best of times, so it was inevitable that I would miss the Beltway exit that would have taken me to my sister's house. I ended up on the wrong side of the city and had to drive through scary neighborhoods to get where I was going.

When the light ahead turned red and the line of cars traveling up New York Avenue stopped, a gaggle of homeless men shuffled off the sidewalk into the street. They began dabbing at windshields with dirty rags, beseeching drivers for money.

I stared at the light, willing it to turn green before they got to me. *This sort of thing doesn't happen in Maine*, I said fretfully to myself. *I'll give them money if I must, but I'd really rather the light just turned green. Come on, light. Turn green. Turn green.*

Then one man turned in my direction. He was making some loud, strange sounds, but he was not begging. His hair stuck out in clumps all over his head. Clad only in a pair of cutoff jeans, he wore no shirt, no shoes. His face and torso were thickly scarred, as if he had been badly burned. He had no arms.

I pressed the button that raised the car windows the last half inch. I checked to make sure the doors were locked. The light turned green, and I drove forward. It wasn't until I was passing under the traffic light that it dawned on me.

"He had no arms," I said aloud.

"What?" the children said.

Shoot. Oh, shoot. "He had no arms," I repeated.

"Who?" Ellie asked me.

"That man back there . . . he had no arms."

"Poor man," said Ellie.

Poor man! He had no arms. He couldn't hurt me. I didn't need my fists, didn't need to flee: What did I have in the car that he might need? What did I have that he might want? Juice boxes, cookies, money, Band-Aids, and baloney . . . *but I checked the door locks and the windows to make sure they were closed against him.*

"Shoot. Oh . . . shoot!"

"Mama is crying," Woolie announced.

Having seen, what could I do? Turn around, go back? Chase him down the street, this poor, differently abled, mentally challenged person of color? *Hey! I can see you now! You're innocent, truly a child of God! Oh, please, can I give you a Fig Newton?*

It was too late. He was gone.

The centurion was surrounded by children of God. Everyone on every cross, the robbers, the bandits, the Jews and the gentiles, each of these was one of God's babies, even if the gospel writers don't waste their tears on anyone but Christ. The only God worth worshipping would shake His earth and tear His hair over the least of these, His fallen sparrows.

If it is obvious enough, the trembling earth occasionally startles us into glimpsing what is true. The centurion looked into the face of the dying Christ, and the Not-See suddenly saw.

What could he do? Undo? Climb the cross, pull out the nails, take the body into his arms? It was too late. The man was dead, by the centurion's own order.

And the grace of God was with him nonetheless, and all around him: saffron light and choirs of angels. Love and praise for this dead and broken god poured from his mouth like music. Not because of who he was but because of *what God is.*

In the museum shop at the National Gallery, I found a postcard of a medieval icon of Jesus on the cross. On the postcard, though not in the original painting, Jesus has a face, a crown of thorns, a torso, but no arms. The arms, which would have extended beyond the edge of the postcard, are amputated right about where the homeless man's arms had been. I keep this picture on the wall above my desk.

Give me the right pitch, God, and I am the Sammy Sosa of love; give me the right visual, and I'll smack that ball out of the park.

Give me a cop in a uniform; give me a mother with four children standing in the Rockland Shop 'n Save, and I can see her and love her like nobody's business. Give me anything else and I . . .

Could too easily be the Not-See or, at best, the centurion before the cross who gets his glimpse too late.

There is the grand, beautiful, unconditional, limitless love we want to give to one another, the love that bears all things, endures all things, *believeth all things,* the love that sees. And then there is the stingy, shabby, nearsighted human love we find ourselves giving. The aching, immeasurable distance between one and the other can be filled only by grace.

PRAYER FOR A GLASS HEART

Blessed is the breath of the glassblower, who
With skilled and steady exhalation
Heats the gritty solid of the heart
And with his breath expands
My heart until a wider vessel is created;
Until my heart's capacity is such
The whole world can be embraced in love. Blessed be!
Even though a heart's walls ache as they expand
Even if glass must, of necessity, grow fragile
To encompass
As it shines.
Allowing light, more light, more light:
May the glassblower breathe and breathe until
With the slightest tap my heart
Flies and shatters into sand.
Blessed be the breath of the glassblower
Craftsman of fragility
Artist of the shatter and the shine.
Amen.

      KB

9

Prayers for Help

The Reverend Margaret Guenther has written in *The Practice of Prayer* that "True prayer, whatever outward form it might take, is first and foremost a condition of loving attentiveness to God in which we find ourselves open and receptive to who we are in our deepest selves."

Another way of phrasing this definition is to say that prayer brings us to greater/broader/higher consciousness—or at least it should. However, if we were to pray, meditate, attend church, or indeed participate in any other outward form of spiritual practice with the sole aim of "find[ing] ourselves open and receptive to who we are in our deepest selves," our practice would fall far short of its potential. Neither God nor evolution established human consciousness purely for the sake of consciousness. Rather, consciousness allows for empathy.

So if the practice of prayer (whatever outward form it might take) encourages us to wake up! pay attention! and become more conscious, it should also, by definition, inspire us to compassion, helpfulness, and empathy. (Here is a quick and handy way to judge the merits of any religion or philosophy, from Sam Harris's atheism to the reforms of Vatican II: Does it seem to make its adherents kinder, more understanding, and helpful? *The tree is known by its fruit*, as the Man said.)

I can't pretend to be unconditionally in favor of the practice of prayer. No, I've got plenty of conditions. I'll pray only as long as prayer helps me to be more present, more aware and attentive, and as long as prayer helps me to see the suffering of others. As long as prayer reminds me to deploy both my resources and my generosity, I'll pray, and I will keep on praying so long as prayer serves as a uniquely potent means of giving and receiving love.

"There are plenty of other potent means of giving love," my son Peter remarks. "Music, for instance."

Absolutely.

If we define love as the earnest desire for the achievement of wholeness by the beloved, it's not difficult to grasp that some really excellent rock and roll could, all things being equal, enhance such wholeness. So would being cured of leprosy.

Nor, probably, would the beloved's wholeness include dropsy (Luke 14:1–6) or a withered hand (Luke 6:6–11). Anyone capable of healing such afflictions (whether miraculously or medically) should go ahead and "git 'er done" and not fiddle around praying. (WWJD? See Luke 13:10–17, in which Jesus heals a woman who was crippled for eighteen years.)

Physical health isn't the only impediment to a person's wholeness, and maybe it isn't even the most important one. Hitler was a radiantly healthy guy, apparently, but if I had to choose, I'd rather have leprosy, two withered hands, and dropsy (whatever that is) than be Hitler. Still, if someone is starving, for God's sake, don't sit around praying: Give him food. (The same goes for water, warmth, rest, and the Heimlich maneuver.) To assert that prayer is always, under all circumstances, the first thing love should do, or even the best that love *can* do, is irresponsible at best and a self-serving lie at worst.

Sometimes, however, it's all we *can* do. Sometimes prayer is all we've got left.

Blessed be ye poor: for yours is the kingdom of God.
Blessed are ye that hunger now, for ye shall be filled.

Blessed are ye that weep now:
For ye shall laugh.
> Luke 6:20–21

Two hundred and fifty thousand people have died in an earthquake in Haiti, hundreds of thousands more are suffering there, of every imaginable torment, and I can't help.

I can't bind up the broken or let captives go free or replace ashes with garlands. I'm in Maine.

I dwell in an intact house, I am warm in a cold climate, and when I turn the tap, clean water pours out.

Other people are headed to Haiti to do the things I can't do—a lot of people, for love is an enormous thing, and the people who devote their lives to it are legion. Doctors Without Borders, UNICEF, Oxfam, Catholic, Jewish, Baptist, and Mennonite relief organizations, Artists for Peace and Justice, and American soldiers are all going to Haiti *in locum tenens*. I send money.

Money doesn't have a particularly good reputation among the devout, who are generally as eager to ascribe virtue to the impoverished as they are to avoid joining their company. But I love the stuff. The best thing about money is that you can use it to bridge a wide geographic gap between lover and beloved and translate compassion into succor over long distances.

This is just as well, since the global media has extended the reach of our senses until we can see, hear, and feel with the suffering all around the world. People have always been subject to flood, famine, and earthquakes, though only recently have there been quite so many witnesses. But there is money, praise be to God. Cash or plastic, we have a way of translating our prayers into aid, the Word into flesh. God bless this greenback: May it be received as it was offered, in the spirit of love.

When my son Zachary was about eight years old, his grandfathers (both veterans) provided him with videos of old World War II movies. He liked these very much and—like generations of small boys before him—would play at being the hero. Aloft on the saw-horse swing, Zach would become John Wayne, fighter pilot, coming in for a landing after a midair dogfight with a Japanese Zero. He'd clamber out of his bullet-ridden aircraft and brush the dust off his breeches.

His brother Peter, following the script, would cry, "Sir! Your plane is full of holes!"

As Zach sauntered off to have a drink at the officers' club, he would throw a casual glance over his shoulder and reply in a laconic growl, "*Termites . . .*"

When he was a little boy, Fred Rogers (Mr. Rogers) likewise watched John Wayne, though he had to go to a theater to see a film in those days. The feature would be preceded by a cartoon and then a newsreel, which, Mr. Rogers reports, was usually pretty awful, especially for a little kid to see. During one particularly heartrending newsreel, Mr. Rogers's mother leaned over to her son. "Look for the helpers," she advised in a whisper.

Lo and behold, in the midst of whatever mayhem was unfolding, little Fred would always be able to find someone—a firefighter, an ambulance driver, a passerby—trying to help.

Bless Mrs. Rogers! What wonderful advice to give a child—comforting and inspiring. I gave her advice to my own children to help them when the news was bad.

For a while, the film Zach liked best was *Midway,* about the decisive 1942 Pacific naval battle. Starring Charlton Heston, it required the hero mostly to grit his teeth and prevail, but because there was a romance as well as a war to sort out, the plot was complex and the movie was long. It was an odd favorite for an eight-year-old.

For the climactic battle scene, the filmmakers used actual footage of the battle. In one of these, a navy chaplain is glimpsed very briefly kneeling beside the body of a crewman on the deck of an aircraft carrier. A fighter jet is taking off, as I recall, and something explodes as the chaplain, unflinching, draws a cross in the air above the dead man's face.

On the morning after one of the first weekend viewings of *Mid-*

way, Zach and Peter went outdoors, as usual, to play. Glancing out of the kitchen window, I saw them together on the lawn. They were kneeling somberly, facing each other above the limp little body of Zach's favorite stuffed bunny. Their heads were bowed, Peter's palms pressed together in prayer, as Zach raised his grubby paw and made a cross in the air, administering last rites to Rab Rab.

Look for the helpers. Become the helpers. Dear, wise Mrs. Rogers!

PRAYER TO BE SAID
AT THE SOUND OF A SIREN

God grant courage to those who suffer;
Strength and peace to those who help.
Amen.

Not surprisingly, given her father's piety, Natasha attended Catholic schools where nuns taught. She told me that whenever her sixth-grade math class was interrupted by the sound of a siren shrieking through the city streets outside, Sister Mary Magdalene would stop everything, turn toward the windows, and instruct her pupils to "pray for those going to help and for those who will be helped."

I suppose that by sixth grade, these Catholic schoolchildren already knew what prayers to say. Still, I'm not sure the words mattered. The essence of the prayer lay as much in the halt and turn as it did in the words.

If you are on the road, you might be required by law to pause in response to a siren and to pull over to the side of the road so the emergency vehicle might pass safely. Even within your own home, you are likely to notice a siren. Like a meal, or bedtime, or crossing the threshold from home into the world, a siren is an obvious signal with intrinsic significance. Someone is suffering. Someone is rushing to help. You couldn't ask for a better reason to pray.

O God I offer the prayers of my heart
For those who are suffering. I don't know their names.
You know their names, and their sufferings are real to you.
Let them become real to me. Let me know how to be with
    them.
If they must suffer, may they know that they are not alone.
May they be clothed with love, fed with love, warmed and
    protected by love.
May they be held in your hands and blessed in your love.
May the dead find their places in memory, may the wounded
    be healed,
May the mourners be comforted. May the morning come when
    all may arise with joy.
Amen.

KB

My friend Laura and I were together on September 11. We are
both ordained ministers—she's an Episcopal priest—and we both
serve as chaplains for first responders. You would think, therefore,
that Laura and I might have been able to come up with a better, or
at least more specific, prayer than this one:

O God
O God
O God
O God
O God
O God
O God

But that was the one we prayed when the towers fell.
Frankly, neither of us wanted to be praying. We wanted to be
doing, helping, or at least present at the scene, standing with the
cops and firefighters, embracing them, encouraging them, wiping
the dust from their faces and the ashes from their hands. Instead,

we sat together on a couch, side by side, in Thomaston, Maine. We couldn't do a damned thing.

So we said, "O God, O God, O God, O God."

I would give my right arm to be the sort of Religious Person who can force a hurricane to turn aside with my prayers, raise the dead, raise the Towers, or at least raise a differently abled person from his wheelchair just by speaking the Word in my human voice. I'd give my left arm, at least, just to believe that people with that kind of power exist.

I once sat next to a Sri Lankan woman on an airplane who told me with perfect confidence that because Catholicism is God's favorite faith, only Catholic prayers were answered and only Catholic villages were spared the crushing inundation of the 2004 East Asian tsunami. When I got home from that trip, I didn't rush to consult the Internet to see whether Catholic villages were disproportionately spared: I didn't have to.

Nothing I believe allows me to change reality when reality is horrible. I wish it did. It would be wonderful to be able to say, "Look, just believe this, say this, do this, *pray this way*, and those giant waves and tall buildings will not break over those you love, the earth will never open beneath their feet, neither shall lethal viruses find a foothold in their flesh." I want to be able to say this and have it be a fact, not a metaphor.

Oh, what I would give to be able to save people in the way that they, we, all of us really want to be saved, even my devout Sri Lankan fellow traveler: *Eternity with you sounds marvelous, God, but if you don't mind, could you, at this moment and in honor of my Catholicism, just keep this plane from falling out of the sky?*

"Abba . . . Father," Jesus prays, despairing, knowing he is to die. Later, suffering on the cross, Jesus spoke words from Psalm 22: "Eloi, eloi, lama sabachthani . . ."

Eloi, eloi—my God, my God, why have you forsaken me?

My friend Annie Kiermier has come to understand that her tears are prayers. "If this is so," she says, "I've done a lot of praying."

Yeah. Me, too.

Sometimes, after praying, I will be able to think of a way to help that hadn't occurred to me before, as if the pause had freed some creativity, courage, and energy. Though I still can find no way to alleviate the suffering, I am better able to follow Mrs. Rogers's advice. I look for the helpers.

As I sat there on the sofa with Laura on September 11, the people who could do something were doing it. Meanwhile, all over the country, all over the world, all sorts of people were doing more or less what Laura and I were doing: sitting there with our sorrow, our pity, our all but unbearable love. Millions of human tongues in thousands of languages were saying, "O God O God O God O God . . ."

Perhaps you, too, remember that day with excruciating clarity. Perhaps you, too, could do nothing then but sit there, letting the news or the images batter your heart. Maybe you responded with something along the same lines.

If so, then you and I have prayed together.

Let your soul lend its ear to every cry of pain
As a lotus bares its heart to drink the morning sun
Let not the fierce sun dry one tear of pain before
You yourself have wiped it from the sufferer's eyes.
But let each burning human tear fall on your heart
And there remain, nor ever brush it off!
Until the pain that caused it is removed.
        Traditional Vedic Meditation

10

Prayers for the Fearful

With the help of friends, mentors, and the practice of prayer, I've arrived at a reasonably workable description of God ("God = Love") and a faith that, whatever the challenge or conflict, the loving path is the right path; the loving way is the right way.

I am wrong quite a lot of the time, but love is always right. As to that, I have perfect faith.

Unless . . . I don't.

My petit mal failures of faith do not require a terrorist attack or an earthquake for a trigger. Most often, it is enough to have one of my children embark upon, or merely threaten to embark upon, a course I have misgivings about. At such times, all faith abandoned, I am perfectly capable of lying awake all night, fretting into the darkness as the hours pass.

What if Zach is smoking pot? What if he keeps it up, what if he graduates from marijuana to stronger, more addictive drugs, what if he ends up like the kids I come across in my work—the dirty, vague, sly, and hopeless ones whose eyes don't track and whose vestigial intelligence is sufficient only to let them be ashamed of what they have become?

Maybe I should piss-test all the children every single day of their young lives just to make sure they never tried drugs . . . What if my child is smoking dope right this minute, the evil weed already sapping his motivation and dulling his intellect? And now he is snowboarding, and a lot of the local kids who snowboard also seem to smoke pot, besides which, I'm sure he takes off the helmet as soon as I'm gone, so I should probably ski behind him and monitor him. But he's a whole lot faster on the snowboard than I am on skis, so he could hurt himself even then, and there would be nothing I could do . . . What can I do?

Luckily, my husband, Simon, understands. He has also been known to do the midnight power-fret. Nowadays—oh, the joy of combined families!—we have six kids between us to fret about. It's a wonder we get any sleep at all.

One of us is usually at least slightly less upset about any particular kid-related episode than the other and so can try, at least, to change the mood. Only when commiseration, analysis, offers of a quickie, or some sage advice have failed to relieve the afflicted partner's suffering will one or the other of us remember ourselves and offer an exhausted suggestion as if it were a novelty: "You know, we could pray!"

> O God be with my darling child
> My dear, charming, impulsive, stormy one
> Hold him for me.
> Free him that he may grow;
> Grow in him
> That he may grow in You.
> May my child be loving and beloved.
> Amen.
>   KB

We do this, Simon and I, and then—astonishing but true—we sleep.

I am a law-enforcement chaplain, a minister, a writer, but whatever roles I play in the wider world, it is pretty hard to regard my own children from any vantage other than that of a mom. I love them—

all seven of them, counting steps and my beautiful daughter-in-law, Erin. I want them to be happy.

To which my son Peter, at least, might say, "Yeah, right!" And remind me of all the times I went out of my way to make him unhappy. Very, very unhappy. Like this time, for example:

Back in the day—we're talking seven or eight years ago now, when he was maybe fourteen—Peter had a friend named Ted. We used to call him Evil Ted, because Peter always got into trouble when Ted was around. Once Peter and Evil Ted sneaked out of the house in the middle of the night, determined to do something stupid. I didn't hear them on the stairs. I didn't hear the back door close softly behind them.

The boys spent the night climbing trees, hurling themselves into drainage ditches, and climbing onto the roof of the high school. At one point, Peter stripped off his clothes and streaked naked around the high school parking lot. After a few more equally intelligent tricks, they got bored and crept home to bed.

Two weeks later, I got a phone call from Evil Ted's father. Turns out Ted's favorite show was called—big surprise, here—*Jackass*. So the boys had not only done all these stupid things, *they'd made a videotape.*

"Teddy is at Disney World this week," Evil Ted's father said. "But I thought you might want to discuss Peter's behavior with him."

"Oh, yes," I said. "I want to discuss it with Peter. He will be over in a few minutes to fetch the tape."

A little while later, following a brief discussion, my darling son appeared at the Thomaston police department. With a bright red face, he handed over a videotape and an invitation: Would the officer on duty please review the tape and then, at her convenience, come over to our house for a meeting?

The bewildered officer agreed. So at three o'clock that very afternoon, Peter ushered the Thomaston officer into our living room, where she joined me and a state trooper. (Why a state trooper? Because I can do these things.)

The police officers sat on the couch, doing their best to look authoritative and stern, while I loaded the videotape into the VCR.

The quality of the videotape wasn't particularly good—it had been nighttime, after all—but the actors and the action were clear enough. There was Evil Ted climbing a tree, there was Peter hurling himself into a drainage ditch. There was the high school parking lot, and there, flying on the wild zephyrs of the night, were the locks of my son's unmistakable red-blond hair as he streaked naked past the camera, the cheeks of his white patootie glowing in the moonlight.

"I'm free, I'm free!" we heard Peter singing in his squeaky, uncertain adolescent voice.

At this point, the state trooper fell prey to a sudden, suspicious fit of coughing, and the Thomaston officer covered her mouth with both hands. So far, the boys had done nothing much worse than risk broken bones and pneumonia.

But then, in irrefutable, grainy videotape, we saw Peter push his way onto a parked school bus, where he urinated copiously on the bus driver's seat. It was a cushioned seat. A paper towel would not right this wrong.

The Thomaston officer and the state trooper scowled. They crossed their arms over their chests and hinted darkly at charges of trespass and criminal mischief.

"Oh, Peter," I said sadly.

Peter's face was pale, his ears bright red. "Am I going to jail?" he whispered.

"I'll have to discuss it with the lieutenant," growled the state trooper.

"Oh, *man*," Peter groaned.

"But before you go to jail, Peter, you have some work to do," I said.

"Do I?" said Peter.

"Today is going to be a very busy day for you."

"Oh, no," said Peter.

"Oh, yes."

The school bus driver, I told him, had been insulted. The school community had been insulted. The community at large had been insulted. Harm had been done that only Peter, as the perpetrator, had the power to heal. "So you will call the principal at the high school. You will call the superintendent of schools. You will confess to each of them, and you will apologize. Then you will go in person to the home of the bus driver—"

"In *person*?"

"—where you will confess, in *person*, and apologize profusely."

"Oh, *man.*"

"Exactly. Oh, man. Then you will write an open letter to the community declaring yourself responsible for this incident, so that suspicion may be lifted from all the other teenagers in the area. You can send it to the editor of the *Courier Gazette*."

"O *God!*"

"And you will scrub the school buses—*all of them*—down to the shine."

"What about Evil Ted?" wailed Peter. "It was his idea!"

"Ted is not my problem," I said. "You are my problem."

"Excuse me, ma'am," said the state trooper, "but aren't you being a little hard on the kid?"

"She's the strictest mother in the whole world," Peter told him glumly.

"Wow," said the trooper. "I guess she is."

Peter spent the next few days working out his sentence. Was he unhappy? Yes. He was unhappy.

Still, the school officials responded to his phone calls with the charmed mercy of people unused to adolescent apologies. The bus driver confided to Peter that he had been a boy once himself. And those spotless school buses garnered compliments and praise.

"I'm all done," Peter announced when, reeking of Mr. Clean, he returned from the last task. "The bus driver said the buses have never looked so good. I hate to admit this, but I feel a lot better."

I may be strict, but I am a mother, after all, and I love my son. I want him to feel good. I want him to be happy.

"I'm glad to hear it," I said.

* * *

Maybe you would disagree with Peter: Maybe the strictest parents in the whole world are reading these lines and thinking of their own offspring with tears in their eyes, remembering what sweet little babies they once were.

When these children were little, those strict parents made them floss their teeth, treat people kindly, say sorry, and clean up when a mess had been made.

My son Peter is an adult now.

Floss or don't floss, treat people as he will, clean up or live with the mess: He's free! He's free!

I don't need to make my son unhappy anymore. He's self-supporting and pays for his own cavities. He has joined me as an adult in the adult world. It's an interesting world, but it is much, much stricter than any parent has either the power or the desire to be.

So what were once his parents' rules have become his parents' prayers:

May you comport yourselves with dignity and treat others and
yourselves with kindness.
May you remember to say "I'm sorry" when it counts
And "I love you" when it's hard to say and therefore matters most.
May you both express and experience thankfulness.

We can't shield our grown son from unhappiness. We can only stand beside him now and bear our confident and loving witness as Peter, in his freedom, applies childhood's lessons to his adult life.

*May this be a life of courage, kindness, and honor. May it be a life
of joy.*
Amen.

As a chaplain, I have witnessed a phenomenon widely recognized by people involved with search-and-rescue operations—namely, that when an ordinarily sensible, intelligent, rational adult gets lost in the woods, he will do uncharacteristically silly things. Suspecting that he might be walking in the wrong direction, *he walks faster.* Until it is so dark that he is literally banging into trees, he does not stop to make a shelter nor inventory his food supply; nor does he consider ways of signaling for help. (Nor, incidentally, does he stop to pray. Perhaps a Getting Lost grace would help?) Signaling for help would be embarrassing. What if he lights a big signal fire and people come running and it turns out he's only a hundred yards from a Wal-Mart? So he presses on. To do anything other than press on would be to admit to himself that he is no longer in control of the situation, and he doesn't want to do that.

When I ask myself why Simon and I, both reasonably intelligent and more or less faith-based people, have to exhaust ourselves with fretting before we finally get around to prayer, the reason seems to be the same—we don't want to admit to our terminal human inadequacy.

So, like the man lost in the Maine woods, we keep going until at last it's so dark, we're banging into trees. Only then do we remember to stop moving, send up a signal, and let ourselves be found.

A prayer inspired by fear implicitly begins with this confession: *I don't know everything. I can't do everything. I am not in control. My children and I are vulnerable to pain.*

It's good to have a prayer handy for when you find yourself in a place that scares you. *O God, O God* is fine for acute situations (and it's all but automatic, anyway). "Thank You" works nicely once you've arrived in safety, even if safety is a Wal-Mart parking lot.

Still, in all but a few circumstances, there is likely to be quite a lot of time between the "O God!" and the "Thank You." For example, if you are lost in the woods, there will be moments in which you might need to eat (see Chapter 3) or sleep (Chapter 4) and so, if you've gotten used to doing so, you'll eventually remember to pray.

What if this mammogram reveals a tumor? What if there's a terrorist on this airplane? What if my kid is a stoner?

Zachary is in the Marine Corps, and he's going to Afghanistan. Over the past decade or so, a few of the game wardens I work with have seen their kids go off to serve in one or the other of our current set of wars. None of these fathers can tell me that it's easy.

"I would watch the news," one of the guys on the dive team told me, "and they would say, 'Two marines killed in Anbar Province.' I knew Jason was in Anbar, so I would start marking time."

"Oh, Phil," I said.

"Yeah. I figured it would take the Corps around three days to make a positive identification of the remains and get someone over here to notify me. So if the fatalities occurred on a Tuesday, I knew I could stop bracing myself and begin to feel okay by, say, Friday or Saturday.

"I shouldn't be telling you this," Phil added. "But it was terrible."

Jason came home. Most of them will come home. Statistically speaking, it's likely.

When Jason came down the exit ramp from the airplane, did Phil and his wife make their baby boy take off his boots and hold out his hands so they could count his fingers and toes?

"On Saturday," Phil was saying, "I would start to feel okay. Then I would think: *Jesus, some other father has been notified by now.*"

In a book called *When Things Fall Apart: Heart Advice for Difficult Times*, the American Buddhist nun Pema Chödrön describes the practice of *tonglen*. The word is Tibetan and means "sending and taking." The practice consists of breathing in the suffering of the world, yielding to the experience of suffering that empathy produces, then breathing out a prayer of compassion, freshness, light, and well-being.

The Tibetans (and Pema Chödrön) practice a form of Buddhism known as Mahayana. Somewhat less sternly purist than Theravada, Mahayana believes in the possibility of the bodhisattva: an enlightened being whose compassion leads her to remain in the endless cycles of birth and death—which her enlightenment allows her to opt out of—able and willing to help others achieve enlightenment. Tibetan Buddhists take the bodhisattva vow of compassion and regularly offer it for all sentient beings:

May all sentient beings be relieved of their pain
May my prayers go out to all sentient beings.

This is a lovely thought. Does it actually do anything, though?

I mean, if a middle-aged woman in the middle of Maine plops down on her tushie, sucks in a breath, and says, "May all sentient beings be relieved of their pain," *are they?* Is even one single sentient being (other than the aforementioned middle-aged Mainer) relieved of pain through prayer?

I want it badly: God! Relieve a sentient being of her pain! While you're at it, keep my boy safe! Keep Phil safe; keep all the game wardens safe, I don't want them to be hurt! Impress upon them, Lord, the need for seat belts and ballistic vests, or maybe . . .

Listen, God. I've got an idea. Why don't you just send them all to Moody's diner tonight?

Moody's used to loan keys to the local cops so that the troopers, wardens, and deputies could stop by the diner in the wee hours, make some coffee, and fry up some eggs to keep them going. I've always loved that image: the uniformed guys standing around holding plates or cups of coffee in their gun hands. No need to keep their backs to a wall, no need to keep their eyes focused on the area of maximum potential threat: They're safe. Safe is good. *Couldn't you send my guys to Moody's tonight, God?*

Greg Richards, Mark Rennington, Tina Griswold, and Ronald Owens were sitting safe together at a coffee shop in Lakewood, Washington, four cops sitting there, doing their paperwork. In their photographs, they look kind and cheerful, so I'm sure they smiled at the baristas, told one another a few jokes, maybe indulged in small boasts about one or another of their nine (total) children.

They were murdered there, gunned down by a man named Maurice Clemmons, who escaped and went on to live for two more days. When recognized by a Seattle police officer, he tried to shoot his fifth cop, but this time the cop shot him. I don't know what Clemmons was doing just before this encounter—that is, what he did in the last minutes of his life. It seems unlikely that he was smiling and laughing with people who loved him. What an awful way to die.

"All I want for Eleanor is that she live . . . and be happy," the child's father told me, and I could only sympathize. I want life and happiness for my children, too.

I pray most fervently for the health and well-being, the longevity and bliss, of my babies. Still, if it were up to me to choose, I would rather be the mother of any one of those fallen Lakewood officers than be the mother of Maurice Clemmons. Even if he had lived.

If my darling twenty-year-old daughter Ellie were not an American college student in the year 2010 but, instead, a German student in 1939, would I ask her to keep her head down, work the system, and join the Party that she might live and prosper? Or would I encourage her to resist, as Sophie Scholl resisted? Sophie Scholl, who, with her brother and friends, discerned the shape and the shame of the Holocaust even as it was unfolding, and did her best to rouse her countrymen to action against the Nazis. She was eventually beheaded by the Nazis for treason. I would proudly be her mother. Righteousness, honor, and integrity are not characteristics to pray for lightly—but they are the ones I pray for, for myself and for my children and, for that matter, for the game wardens I work with. After all, I love them, too.

To love someone—to earnestly desire his or her achievement of wholeness—is to desire more than the longest possible life on earth for him or her. It is also to want more for him or her than pleasure, peace, or prosperity, however nice those things may be. Because we are not perfect and because our own desire for the safety of those we care for may overwhelm our sense of justice or duty, the Christian concludes a petitionary prayer with "Not my will but Thine, Lord." Some mutter this phrase as a way of acknowledging the superior power of an apparently capricious and inattentive deity, but to me, it is a reminder of what I know and accept as true: that love is always and everywhere the highest priority, even when (especially when) the demands of love are not congruent with my desire for safety and contentment. That knowledge and acceptance may not be reflected in the words of my petition: *O God, hear my voice, heal my body, save my child, preserve my game wardens,* but love shall be named in the end. *Amen—may it be so.*

The answer to the question "What use is prayer?" depends on what you identify as the problem you would like prayer to solve.

Because we live in a Christian culture, we consider it a given that what every human being fears above all else is death. Therefore, it stands to reason that what every human being must desire above all else is no death, or endless life. Americans and Europeans are often surprised to learn that there are quite a few world religions that do not offer what "all human beings" want. Taken all together, the adherents of death-fearing faiths—Christianity, Spiritualism, Islam—are probably outnumbered by the ones to whom death really isn't that big a deal.

These include nearly all forms of traditional Judaism, the vastly varied forms of Hinduism, and most kinds of Buddhism. The Jews in the Bible are concerned with—almost obsessed by—the value of life, but it is life here on earth, particularly the righteous life of the community as a whole, rather than a personal life in heaven that they aim for.

In addition (and contrary to popular belief), nirvana is not the Buddhist equivalent of the Muslim's paradise or the Christian's Great By-and-By. It's not a place where the good shall go, bringing along their earthly personalities if not their earthly possessions, to be reunited with loved ones and given face time with God.

Nirvana is very nearly the opposite. In nirvana, the seeker is finally liberated—after diligent practice that often extends over several human lifetimes—from all the temporal and temporary things he ordinarily clings to, including the body, objects, relationships, and even personality (which the Buddha considered to be a mere bundle of illusions).

There is one universal human problem associated with death, of course: It hurts like hell to be the one left behind. King David's lamentations at the death of his friend Jonathan are particularly poignant, and it must squeeze any mother's heart to read of "Rachel, weeping for her children . . . for her children are no more."

When it was my turn to mourn, I took comfort from these stories and this brief, unpretentious story set in a Zen monastery:

An elder of a certain monastery died. On the morning after his death, one of the monastery's eager, new disciples went out into the garden. There, he was astounded to find the monastery's most illustrious teacher weeping beside the dead man's grave.

"Master!" the disciple exclaimed. "You have taught me that suffering arises from attachment . . . that our practice of Zen allows for perfect equanimity . . . that enlightenment comes only when one lets go of all that is impermanent . . . you, who have achieved enlightenment, why, Master, are you weeping?"

"I weep," the master said simply, "because my friend is dead."

As a chaplain, I spend a lot of time in the presence of dead people and living people for whom love has been painfully transmuted into mourning. Perhaps I have been overexposed to death and so too readily accept its inevitability and its apparent finality. Still, the fact remains that all of us will die, and everyone we love will die. This has been true as long as there have been living creatures and will continue to be true until the last remaining virus calls it quits.

Paradoxically, however, our focus on death as the most significant existential human problem gives death far too much credit. Not only does "conquer death" not top the to-do list for many (perhaps most) deities, saviors, and saints, our own behavior flatly contradicts the notion that human beings are afraid to die.

Sure, we're a little creeped out by death in the abstract, and if a lion appeared in the backyard, we'd probably run away. Still, we smoke, drink and drive, bungee-jump, and hang glide; we ride motorcycles, run with the bulls at Pamplona, and own handguns. We experiment with drugs, sadomasochism, and martyrdom, and every year a substantial number of us volunteer outright for immediate decease.

If I may say so, the best moments in any religion's history, Christianity included, have not been rooted in a fear of death. Instead, such moments come when we turn our attention to a real problem—consciousness—that really does vex all humanity (and maybe a few chimpanzees as well).

Consciousness renders us capable of at least a basic empathy. Consciousness is interesting, and empathy is useful, yet these twin capacities cause human beings considerable existential discomfort. It is often painful to be attentive, and excruciating to "feel with" others, since sentient beings have a terrible tendency to suffer.

Closing down consciousness (with drugs, alcohol, or various forms of bigoted Not-Seeing) can help, but the price of that solution tends to be pretty high.

If the best answer sounds crazy to you, join the club: It sounded nutso at first to the Israelites, to the denizens of Nazareth and Jerusalem, to Siddhartha's disciples at Sarnath, and to anyone who has ever watched a Sufi dervish whirl. But it isn't crazy, just—again—paradoxical: The way to manage the miseries of consciousness and the agonies of empathy is to become *more conscious* and thus *more empathetic.* "As you do the practice [of Tonglen], gradually, over time, your compassion naturally expands," Pema Chödrön assures us, "and so does your realization that things are not as solid as you thought. As you do this practice, at your own pace, you'll be surprised to find yourself more and more able *to be there for others* [emphasis added], even in what seemed like impossible situations."

Enlightenment, should you be so disciplined or blessed to attain it, will not subtract pain from your experience. If a friend suffers, you will fret, and if a friend dies, you will weep. Even Jesus wept with Mary because his friend—her brother Lazarus—was dead.

That two-word sentence—"Jesus wept"—is puzzling. Jesus didn't weep when he first heard the news. Indeed, he expressed some enthusiasm, considering it a fine opportunity for a demonstration of God's glory. He even delayed his trip to Bethany, in Judea, where Martha and Mary grieved, to make sure that Lazarus would be entombed long enough to be clearly, even odiferously, dead. ("It's been four days," the mourners protest when Jesus asks that the tomb be opened. "He'll stink.")

Jesus clearly is possessed of an absolute certainty, expressed in his recitation to Martha, whom he meets first on the road to Bethany. "I am the resurrection and the life. Those who believe in me, even though they die, will live, and everyone who lives and believes in me will never die."

Jesus obviously believes this and, moreover, is confidently (and correctly, as it turns out) planning Lazarus's imminent return to life—not the invisible heavenly life in the Father's House of Many Mansions, mind you, but that familiar laugh-and-cry, eat-and-poop, smooch-and-smack life everyone prefers, if they are willing to admit it, to any other on offer.

Jesus has no reason to cry. He won't have to miss Lazarus, won't have his sleep forestalled by the wrenching contractions of his heart, won't have to wake up to a dawn that can bring no relief but only the fresh realization of his loss. He loses nothing: Lazarus shall live!

When Mary came to where Jesus was and saw him, she knelt at his feet and said to him, "Lord, if you had been here, my brother would not have died." When Jesus saw her weeping, and the Jews who came with her also weeping, he was greatly disturbed in spirit and deeply moved . . . Jesus began to weep.

If we take the Christian witness seriously, Jesus was as completely conscious, attentive, and aware as any fully human being can be. In Buddhist terms, he was Enlightened. Did he weep like the Zen monk in the story simply because his friend was dead? Or did Jesus weep because, being fully conscious, he was likewise and by definition empathetic, incapable of doing other than "feeling with" Mary and the others who were in pain?

"I don't know what I would have done if Jason . . ." Phil can't finish the sentence; I know what he was about to say. I think, *Boy, if I imagine I can understand such feelings now, just wait until it's Zach over there. Wait until it's my baby boy with all the other baby boys and girls, Americans, Afghanis, Iraqis, Kurds . . .*

But Phil is lost in a vivid recollection of hard, hard times. I am his chaplain. "I know," I say (although I don't yet.) "It would have been terrible. All I can say is: We would have been there to help you."

Phil nods. When bad things happen, loving people show up to help. (Phil is one of them, after all.) "That's true," he says.

He seems to derive some retroactive comfort from this reminder, and I, by the by, have managed to extract a bit of prophylactic comfort for myself. "If anything bad were to hap—"

Never mind. I still can't finish the thought. And I don't know what I would do, either. But God is love—that I am sure of—and love will stay beside my son in Afghanistan, or Iraq, or wherever he goes. Love will be with me, too. We might not be able to do this together, but neither of us has to do it alone.

I like scripture that's brief and to the point, so *God is love* is one of my favorite lines in the Bible. I like this one, too: *Jesus wept.*

Those two words are the entirety of Verse 35 of the eleventh chapter of the Gospel of John.

Chapter 11 is often read at funerals, though the minister usually wraps up the reading about ten verses sooner, in 11:25–26. That's when Jesus declares, *"I am the resurrection and the life. . . ."*

It was and remains a speech meant to comfort, and perhaps it does comfort some. Martha's response to Jesus' declaration presumably expresses relief, not mere obedience.

When I grieve, I grieve like Mary, down on my knees and faithless with fury. When it is up to me to read John's gospel at a funeral, I let the story run on through those additional ten verses, in case there are others who can find no relief or refuge (yet?) in theological abstractions. Let us also be offered this image of a Savior, fully human, fully divine, the man who kneels with us in the dust and allows the tears to be his prayers.

It takes courage to love a human being, courage to risk loving a person made of stardust, rain, and air, courage to recognize her human finitude and trust nonetheless in the infinity of love.

Grief is love. The physical pain, anguish, yearning rage: All of this is love. If we are among the fortunate—the ones who love and live long enough—each of us will take a turn at this particular mode of love. Because it is love, grief can be trusted. It is not, in itself, mental illness (although, because it demands so much effort, it can make us more vulnerable to mental and physical illness), and it is not, in itself, traumatic or damaging to a human being.

Death is, after all, not merely a possibility or even a probability but the one event every living being back to the first blob of slime could count on. If it is your turn, let grief be your whole work; know it to be the fullness of your obligation to God and to the world for now.

If it is not your own loss that moves your heart to prayer but, rather, a loss that has come to someone you care for, prayer need not be the very first priority. Or perhaps we might say that if there is ever a time for prayer to take some other form than words, it is the moment when a friend is broken by grief. That is when our prayers are offered with our tears, our arms, the sounds we make with our mouths and throats that say nothing more than "I am with you." Such moments will continue to occur, incidentally, as the loss announces itself in all the unwelcome novelties of the mourner's new life: the bed that no longer holds a husband, a small spoon no longer needed to feed the baby, a ringing telephone that will never again serve as prelude to a mother's voice.

Once the impact has been absorbed (again), the tumult abated (again), and the bereaved has again struggled upright in one of the unheralded, reliable, and nonetheless miraculous resurrections performed by the human spirit, a prayer can be offered on his or her behalf.

PRAYER AFTER WEEPING

O God whose work and will and very name is love we thank You
for the gift we were given in [name].

We yield with confidence to grief, knowing that pain will pass and
   sorrow ends, but love does not die and will not end.
Love abides in us, around us, and beyond us, forever and ever.
Thanks be to God.
Amen.

11

Prayers Before Offering Service

Father Mychal Judge, OFM, the devout, gay, recovering-alcoholic Catholic priest and chaplain to the New York City Fire Department, died with the firefighters he served on September 11.

As a chaplain, I turn often to Father Mychal's example for inspiration, and a prayer he wrote has become the threshold prayer I say before I go to work.

Whether you are a bystander called to help or a professional provider of care, it is normal to respond to an unfamiliar or unexpected crisis with bewilderment and fear. One of the strongest fears we have is that of making things worse. It prevents us from doing all sorts of difficult, good, and loving things: showing up at funerals, bringing food or flowers to the bereaved, staying by a friend's bedside when the oncologist comes in with the news.

Father Mychal responded to these feelings in himself with this prayer:

Lord, take me where you want me to go
Let me meet whom you want me to meet
Tell me what you want me to say
And keep me out of your way.

I have a postcard on my wall that shows Father Mychal as an icon, painted in his Franciscan robes, a white FDNY helmet clasped under his arm, a halo around his head, and his right hand held up in a gesture of blessing. If a crisis is moving swiftly, and I don't have the time or brain room for even a silent recitation of Father Mychal's words, his picture will pop into my head like a Power-Point slide, and the spirit of the prayer, if not the prayer itself, will be with me.

One of the first things a chaplain has to learn is that his job is often simply to show up (at the fire, the hospital bedside, the hostage situation, the suicidal student's dorm) and allow God (or the lieutenant) to decide what use to make of him.

For ministers who trained for church ministry, it can be strange to have so little direction, authority, or control, and also to have so little practical importance compared with the firefighters going into the black smoke to find survivors, or the divers slipping under the ice to retrieve a body.

To me, the most important line is the last one: "Keep me out of your way." *Oh! May I not prove to be an obstacle between these workers and the miracle of love. May I be transparent, vanish! so that your light may shine through me. But if I can't make things better, God, please, please, don't let me make things worse.*

A miracle has to be both perceptible (at least to those people willing to perceive) and meaningful. A miracle can provoke awe, but it must provoke gratitude. (*Wow! Thank you!*) Otherwise, it's just a magic trick.

When presented with a man who was "blind from birth," Jesus didn't give the guy purple hair just because he could. Instead, Jesus spat on the ground, mixed up some mud, and smeared it on the blind man's eyes. The man went off, washed up, and thereafter boasted gratefully of perfect vision.

All other things being equal, we can probably agree that being blind is not a good thing. Wouldn't it be great if the blind could be allowed to see the smiles of those they love? And while we're at it, wouldn't it be great if the deaf could enter into the world of Mozart and birdsong, while the halt and the lame (soldiers returning from wars with spinal cord injuries, for example) could kick up their heels and dance?

Jesus does what anyone with a truly good and loving heart would do if only he or she had the power to do it. This is likely the point—or at least one of the points—of the gospel story.

WWJD, as the bumper sticker puts it. What would Jesus do?

What actions are most excellent?
To gladden the heart of a human being
To feed the hungry
To help the afflicted
To lighten the sorrow of the sorrowful
To remove the wrongs of the injured.
That person is most beloved of God
Who does the most good to God's creatures.
> The Prophet Muhammad

Neurologist and author Oliver Sacks has written about a man born blind whose sight was restored. This miracle occurred neither through prayer, nor through a concoction of dirt and divine saliva, but through the surgical correction of the patient's eyes.

The blind man had agreed eagerly to the surgery, experimental and delicate though it was. The operation went well, although the man's eyes had to be bandaged for a time to let them heal, but at last the day came when the bandages could be removed. The surgical team, the man's family, and others assembled as the nurses carefully unwound the dressings from the patient's face. All were hushed, expectant.

For the first time in his life, the man opened his eyes and . . .

What were they expecting? What would you expect?

Jubilation! Joy! "Ah, color! Light! My wife's sweet face, just as I'd always imagined it!" Instead, the man turned his head from side to side. His expression was baffled and frightened.

"What's wrong?" the doctor asked at last, and at the sound of his voice, the man turned in his direction.

"Oh, my God!" he said, his voice trembling. "I thought I was all alone." And the man began to weep.

The man had been blind since birth. His brain knew only sound and touch, smell and taste; it had never received visual stimulation. It had never developed the neural pathways needed for processing visual images and had never created the categories by which he might understand the data now crashing against his retinas on waves of light. Technically, his eyes worked—but he could not make sense of what he saw.

The heartbreaking thing is, he never could learn to make sense of it. His brain could not adjust to process vision, so the visible world never became comprehensible, let alone beautiful, to this poor man. It was always a bright, confused madness hovering in front of him. He became profoundly depressed and begged the doctors to reblind him. When they would not, he could find relief only in blindfolding himself and living in darkness, artificially returning to the one world in which he could function.

Let's say you are a good, kind, and loving person, called by God or compelled by your own human love to do good, kind, and loving things. You open your heart to the sufferers whom God places in your path, you love them, and you work hard to alleviate their suffering.

Forget for a moment the strenuous absurdity of trying to be virtuous in a culture that demands and rewards selfishness. How ridiculous is it that those who manage to tamp down, if temporarily, the Whac-A-Mole demands of their own egos and reach out to others can find they have made the situation and the suffering *worse*?

Ask an animal lover.

My mother and I were driving together near her farm in Maryland when we saw a box tortoise crawling across the road in the endearingly dim, determined manner of its kind. My mother pulled over and stopped. We were of one mind: We would save this tortoise from being squashed on the busy roadway.

My first thought, as I alighted, was that the tortoise had a specific destination, and I would simply provide transportation across the perilous asphalt to the rough grass on the other side.

As I scooped up the tortoise, it gave an indignant wheeze and swiftly retracted its limbs and head, bringing up the hinged piece of plastron that closes the brown-and-butterscotch patterned "box" of protective shell.

"I have an idea," my mother called from the car. "Why don't we bring it home to show the kids, and then it can live in my garden?"

One could make an argument that the tortoise had its own life to live, its own agenda that we were proposing to interrupt. On the other hand, box tortoises are not known for sentimentality, my children had never seen a box tortoise up close, and my mother's garden was part of a large farm with plenty of wetland and woods forming prime habitat for all sorts of wildlife. Surely this tortoise would prefer paradise to the verge of a state highway.

So we went on our way with the box tortoise riding on the floor of the car between my feet. Curiosity eventually overcame caution, and the tortoise thrust its head out of its shell, its wrinkled neck giving it the appearance of a hawk-nosed retiree. Legs emerged, and the tortoise began exploring the area around my feet. I glanced down at it now and then, but it seemed in no imminent danger of either escape or of getting wedged under my seat.

After a while, however, I glanced down at the tortoise and noticed something I hadn't seen before. "Mom," I said. "There's something wrong with the tortoise's eye."

"What?"

"The tortoise's eye."

"What's wrong with it?"

"I just noticed that there's a . . . worm in its eye," I said. And such is the power of a seminary education that I automatically added silently, *And there's a beam in my eye, too.*

"Oh," said Mom.

We considered this problem while the tortoise investigated my bootlace. "We could bring it back to where we found it and let it go," I suggested.

"We could," Mom agreed. "But it's an awfully long way back, and I'm not sure I would know exactly where we stopped. Besides, we don't want the poor thing to die of . . . well, of whatever's wrong with it."

"I'm not sure the kids are going to be enthusiastic about seeing a box tortoise with a maggot coming out of its eyeball," I said.

"Wait!" said Mom. "We'll be going right by the vet's office: We'll just stop in and let Dr. Carr take a look. Maybe he can cure it?"

So we handed the box tortoise over to the veterinarian, who anesthetized it, examined the eye, decided that the ailment, whatever it was, would ultimately prove fatal. He put it to sleep.

And so, at the cost of several gallons of extra gas and $275 in veterinary fees, a tortoise who had been going along minding its own business was plucked out of its familiar habitat and treated to any number of incomprehensible, alarming, and probably painful procedures (how, for example, is anesthesia administered to a box tortoise?), before meeting the inevitable. If death was inevitable, being squashed on the road would have been far less stressful.

Our intentions were good, but the outcome was almost certainly worse than it would have been without our help.

In March 1989 the oil tanker *Exxon Valdez* ran aground in Alaska, spilling millions of gallons of crude oil into Prince William Sound. The media showed heartbreaking photographs of black, smothered beaches, oil-coated cormorants unable to fly, and sea otters clawing in agony at their oil-filled eyes and screaming in pain from their oil-dried, cracked, inflamed skin.

Volunteers left their work and family obligations and went to Alaska, where clinics were established to help the suffering animals. The work of cleaning oil from the otters' fur and bodies was difficult and time-consuming. Kind, good, and loving work so often is. But while this work saved some animals, the survivors were plagued by long-term health problems; oil is a persistent toxin. Duka, a rescued sea otter, lived until May 30, 2010, in Seattle, and oiled sea otters would not survive at all without human intervention. More recently, crews involved in helping clean up the even bigger Gulf oil spill are experiencing their own health problems as a result of their good work.

We live in a universe rife with irony.

Ask a person committed to economic justice.

In the Mariana Islands, international exposure of the scandalous exploitation of sweatshop labor forced large international corporations to withdraw their business. It was a victory for right-thinking American and Western European consumers, who can now purchase Gap and Tommy Hilfiger clothing guilt-free (more or less).

A friend of mine recently visited the islands to investigate the aftermath of this triumph of virtue. The seamstresses and garment workers who had worked in the sweatshops were primarily female. When the big corporations pulled out, the demand for their sewing skills vanished. Sex tourism swiftly replaced the sweatshop as the primary employer of female labor. The women who once supported their families by sewing now sell their bodies to men who, like the corporations before them, travel to these islands to obtain services that are either more expensive or completely unavailable back in Japan, Russia, or Korea. I will leave it to your tender imaginations what such services might be.

What would Jesus do?

Jesus would do exactly the right thing, for the right reasons, to the right people and—more to the point—get the right results every time. Easy enough for him: He's *divine,* for Christ's sake! Omnipotent, omniscient, omnicompetent, perfect.

So Jesus could wave his hand over an oil-poisoned cormorant, and the cormorant, like a first-century leper, would be made clean. Jesus could lose his temper, knock over the tables in the sweatshops, sweep all iniquity before him, and the former garment workers would come out ahead, living ever after in dignified prosperity.

We're fully human, as Jesus was, but we aren't divine. Even our best efforts at loving our neighbors as ourselves are compromised by our own lamentable ignorance, by our manifold weaknesses, and by the lack of a perspective that God and only God could possibly command. So we can't guarantee that our best attempts at making miracles won't backfire and make a mess instead.

I, by my works, will show you my faith, says the Letter of James. Sometimes that's just what I'm afraid of.

And still, all around us, sentient beings are suffering. Human empathy, divine sympathy, or some conspiracy between the two gives rise to a command within the human heart that cannot go unanswered. *Do something. Help.*

Ask a nurse or a doctor. Ask a cop.

When I first began working as a minister, I was nervous in the pulpit. I used to hide my hands under the lectern, and as I preached, my twitching fingers would be shredding paper into smaller and smaller bits. By the time the service ended, I would have a little pile of what looked like fine snow under there.

I used to reassure myself, in the stomach-churning lead-up to the sermon, that nothing truly terrible would happen if I *preached wrong.* If I lost control in the middle of a church service, I could embarrass myself and ruin your Sunday morning, but if the cop I had coffee with after the service were to screw up, he could kill an innocent person or be killed by a guilty one.

One way to handle the existential problem of being called to do good when not only the world but you yourself are terminally imperfect is to confine yourself to predictable acts of kindness, small, safe, sensible acts of beauty. After all, the more potential your actions have to do a grand and glorious good, the more possibilities there will be for failure, confusion, hurt, and harm.

However, we are not called to love the Lord our God with half a heart, part of a mind, or a smidge of spirit: To truly love our neighbors as ourselves must be to *risk ourselves.* It is a real and frightening risk that some accept simply by virtue of the jobs they choose to do.

Imagine yourself—confronted by suffering. Maybe you're tired or distracted or frightened, and the sufferer you're looking at looks exactly like all the other people of this type whom you've seen a thousand times before. You are going to do something for or to him. You have to do something. It's your job. You can't walk away.

So you make a wrong diagnosis, you administer the wrong medication, you see a gun where you should have seen a wallet, you search the left hiking trail first, and the diabetic child on the right slips into a coma.

These are irreparable, unbearable mistakes that a loving heart would carry as pain and shame forever. But what if no one were willing to risk it?

I, like many of my colleagues, pray a version of this before every sermon.

> May the words of my mouth
> And the meditations of my heart
> Be acceptable to you, my Lord and my God,
> My strength and my redeemer.

There's no paper snow under my pulpit these days, but I won't ever be entirely free of nervousness. It emerges from a desire to preach well, to love well, and to do it right. We are—all of us, whatever our work—called to love God and neighbor, heart and mind and soul. We are all called to risk too much by loving too much.

So say your prayers and then perform your service. Do this as bravely, sensibly, and lovingly as you can, and let the outcome rest in the hands of God. This is the best any of us can do. It is all we need to do. It is enough.

> Let nothing disturb you
> Let nothing frighten you

All things pass away:
God never changes
Patience obtains all things.
He who has God
Finds he lacks nothing.
God alone suffices.

St. Teresa of Ávila

12

Laughter and Prayer

Contrary to anything you might expect, people who have experienced the unexpected death of someone they love are capable of laughter—even quite soon after receiving the news. It is surprising and somehow heartening to see how quickly a person's sense of humor resurrects, declaring the underlying vitality and essential integrity of the bereaved.

One summer day, by a lake in central Maine, I stood beside a woman whose husband had drowned. His body had only just been recovered.

The woman was perhaps sixty-five. She and her husband had been married a long time. The game wardens brought his body ashore, zipped in a body bag. His wife wanted to see it before the waiting hearse took it away.

Together, she and I knelt in the grass. She held her husband's hands between her own, neatened up his bright red shirt, and smoothed the thin wet hair back from his calm forehead. This took a little while. The wardens waited patiently.

"He looks beautiful," I said sincerely.

"Yes. He always was pretty handsome," his wife agreed. "Although," she went on, smiling some and tugging his collar gently into place, "I've never really liked this shirt." We laughed a very little bit. Then we prayed. *"The Lord is my shepherd . . ."*

Funny, how different lines pop out of the Twenty-third Psalm depending on the circumstances. There we were, the new widow and I, with the still and shining waters of the lake before us and a bona fide green pasture behind, and in between, love. The love that brings two together in a happy and humorous marriage, the love that brings them into communion with the natural world, the love that inspires game wardens to respond to calamity with capable compassion and then to stand quietly in the presence of grief.

My cup runneth over. Or, anyway, my eyes do, and the new widow hands me a Kleenex.

The fearful journey between "Yes" and "Thank You" can be long, dark, and hard. Still, I am glad to report that, along with meals and songs, it seems there will also, almost certainly, be *laughter* along the way.

I'd been in the dentist's chair often in the weeks leading up to Christmas, getting various excruciating and expensive things done inside my mouth and paying back all that valuable time I'd saved as a youngster by not flossing. I was getting a real feel for my dentist's sense of humor, though I had not yet begun to share it.

"Did you hear the one about the dyslexic rabbi?" my dentist asked me. "He walks around saying 'YO'!"

He also had amusing motivational posters stuck on his ceiling with Scotch tape, which by then I'd memorized. A kitten dangling from a tree branch has a thought balloon coming out of its little head that says, HANG IN THERE, BABY! FRIDAY'S COMING. A couple of parrots are on a toboggan (FRIENDS DON'T LET FRIENDS DO STUPID THINGS ALONE!). And a glum pug is saying, TODAY IS THE TOMORROW YOU WORRIED ABOUT YESTERDAY.

The one that struck me as particularly interesting on this particular day was of a chimpanzee grinning at the camera with a thought balloon right behind its furry little head that says, DON'T WORRY. BE HAPPY.

My first thought was that "Don't worry, be happy" was cruel

advice to foist upon a person who was giving herself a gum graft for Christmas.

But my second reaction—typical me—was to point out to my dentist that, from a primatological perspective, the poster was inaccurate and misleading. Or at least I tried to point this out. It is difficult to say the words "primatological perspective" with that doohickey slurping away in the corner of your mouth. The information I actually conveyed sounded something like "My mother is Palestinian."

The dentist nodded. He was preparing an enormous steel syringe. "A man walked into a bar," he said. "It hurt."

Human beings share about 98 percent of their DNA with chimpanzees, and biologist Jared Diamond has claimed that Homo sapiens should really be classified as a species of chimpanzee, given that we are closer in our DNA to chimps (whether Pan troglodytes or Pan paniscus, the Bonobo) than a horse is to a zebra or, indeed, than an African elephant is to an Indian elephant.

The similarities between us and these wild animals are clear and often charming: Chimps create tools out of rocks and twigs; they instruct their young and others in tool use; they sympathize and empathize, and, it seems, they mourn their dead. Less appealingly but just as familiarly, chimps use violence and rape as a means of territorial expansion.

Captive chimps can be taught to use sign language, and they have been shown to engage in deliberate deceit, which is to say, chimps know how to lie.

Therefore, my cousin was grinning at me from my dentist's ceiling. Her fetching smile was not, however, a sign of worry-free joy. A chimpanzee's "grin" (exploited by circuses and Hollywood as well as by the makers of motivational posters) is its anxiety or fear face.

A dentist is a man of science, isn't he? How is it, I wanted to ask, that human beings have diverged so significantly in evolution from the ancestor we share with chimps that a human smile anticipates a laugh and is a sign of joy and welcome, not to mention Christmas cheer? (Chimpanzees laugh, incidentally, but they do it by panting: not "Ho ho ho" but "Oh oh oh." Are they the dyslexics, or are we?)

"Are you afraid of Christmas?" my dentist was saying as he fired up his drill. "Maybe you are Santa Claustrophobic . . ."

My nephew Quintus once asked his mother why Santa is always shown laughing "Ho ho ho" as he flies off on his sleigh. Before my sister could answer, Quintus said darkly: "Maybe he's laughing at all the bad kids who aren't going to get what they wanted for Christmas."

Quintus, who at times has had reason to assume he was on the "naughty" list, had no trouble imagining a Santa who not only withholds gifts from the undeserving but sniggers at them, too. After all, there is much human laughter that is cruel or wicked. Ask Wile E. Coyote, ask Elmer Fudd, ask the Three Stooges or Jim Carrey, whose great gag in nearly every movie seems to involve being kicked in the crotch.

Maybe the biblical story of Job, who has all the horrible things happen to him, was supposed to be a comedy.

This isn't as far-fetched as it might seem: Not long after my first husband died, I drove down to Maryland to visit my mother on her farm. I hadn't been there longer than two hours when I accidentally stepped on a pitchfork, and it went through my foot. Technically, I should say, it wasn't a pitchfork but a dung fork, and I was standing in dung at the time, which meant there was dung inside my foot.

So I wrapped my filthy foot in a towel, and my mother drove me to the emergency room in her farm truck, and we laughed like ninnies the whole way there. Why? Because I was a newly widowed mother of four young children, and I had a dung fork through my foot.

Cops are famous for dark humor. You wouldn't believe the moments in which I, as a law-enforcement chaplain, have laughed with cops, or the things I've laughed about. On the other hand, you might easily believe it if you happen to be employed in emergency medicine, firefighting, or have ever been in a war. In Afghanistan, it has been reported, children laugh when they hear the characteristic whine of mortar rounds flying overhead.

So maybe a human smile, too, is a fear face?

REMEMBER THE REASON FOR THE SEASON! read the marquee of a church I passed the other day, helpfully suggesting I read the Gospel according to Luke, 1:26–38. Underneath, black letters spelled out HO HO HO!

Does anybody "ho ho ho" in the Gospels?

Actually, there are a few characters in the Bible who have a sense of humor. Check out Genesis 18, for example: In that story, God's messengers have turned up in Abraham's dooryard to inform him that his wife, Sarah, is going to become pregnant.

Now, Abraham and Sarah were old, advanced in age, it had ceased to be with Sarah after the manner of women. So Sarah laughed, saying, "After I have grown old, and my husband is old, shall I have pleasure?"

The Lord said to Abraham, "Why did Sarah laugh?"

"I didn't laugh," says Sarah.

"Oh, yes, you did laugh!"

(God is a little offended, I think. No one, not my nephew Quintus and not God, likes to be laughed at.)

At ninety, Sarah was unquestionably a woman whom a modern obstetrician would call an elderly primigravida, a term that includes all women over thirty-five—not just nonagenarians. She would eventually commemorate her reaction to the news of this impending geriatric parturition by naming the newborn Isaac, which means "I laughed." She isn't laughing because she's going to bear the promised child, progenitor of a chosen people. No, according to the text, Sarah cracks up because the idea of doing the wild thing with ol' Abraham is just . . . hysterical.

"You'll like this one, Kate." The dentist was fitting an instrument that looked like a meat tenderizer onto the end of his drill. "How does a Mexican law-enforcement officer say 'Merry Christmas'?"

"????!"

"Police Navidad." He giggled happily to himself, and his drill growled.

On the ceiling, a fluffy baby duck stands in front of a suspiciously clean eggshell. THE EGG MUST BREAK BEFORE THE BIRD CAN FLY. (Comrade Lenin said that, didn't he?)

A pastor asked a little boy if he said his prayers every night.

Politely, the boy answered, "Yes, ma'am."

"And do you always say them in the morning, too?" the pastor asked.

"No, ma'am," the boy replied, "I'm not scared in the daytime."

I don't know if the story of Job is meant to be funny, but I am almost positive that the story of Sarah is.

Picture Sarah standing in the shadow of the tent entrance. She's lived a long (*long!*) life with an exasperating husband and plenty of headaches and disappointments. And now God tells her that she's going to have a baby. At the age of ninety.

Have you ever been told you're going to have a baby when you weren't actually expecting the news? (I have. Four times.)

Sarah has to be a little freaked out, right? And so she laughs.

Humor is a prelude to faith. Laughter is the beginning of prayer. Remember the reason for the season? Luke 1:28–34 tells us of the announcement of another absurd, impossible pregnancy:

—God's messenger came to Mary and said "Greetings, favored one! The Lord is with you."

But she was confused and frightened by his words . . .

The angel said to her "Do not be afraid, Mary, for you have found favor with God. And now you will conceive in your womb and bear a son, and you will name him Jesus. He will be great and will be called the Son of the Most High, and the Lord God will give to him the throne of his ancestor David. He will reign over the house of Jacob forever, and of his kingdom there will be no end."

Mary said to the angel: "How can this be, since I have not been with a man?"

As in the story of Sarah and Isaac, in this story there is fear, and why not? This was news that came out of the blue (if Gabriel was the variety of angel who flaps around in the sky). Where there is fear, look for laughter.

The word translated as "to be with a man" is the Greek *gynoskos,* which means "to know." The King James Version retains the literal meaning ("How shall this be, seeing I know not a man?"), while the translators who produced the *New Oxford Bible* give Mary's words as "How can this be, since I am a virgin?" This is the gist of what she is saying, but their translation takes the punch out of the punch line. Then, as now, "to know" could be used as slang for sexual intercourse. So Mary actually answered the angel's long-winded divine pronouncement with a variant of Sarah's frank and rather earthy question: "How can I be pregnant, if I have never had sex?" Try it in a Monty Python accent. Or with the voice of a Valley Girl. It definitely works as a laugh line.

Is there laughter in the Kingdom of God? Only if fear is also there.

Ho ho ho! Jesus was born and Christmas scheduled during a scary time of year when darkness falls early, exposing all those cold, uncaring stars that gleam beyond the thinning membrane of our atmosphere. For all our carols, chants, and incantations, for all our lighting of candles and ringing of bells, maybe this will be the solstice when the sun never really does come back.

Christmas is also scary because this is a season of love, and to love is to risk.

What if our love is not enough, what if it isn't returned, what if we cast our hearts into the world only to reel them in broken? God put God's heart into the world, the Christmas story goes, in the form of an infant born wet into winter air. Look what happened to him.

Ho ho ho, and here comes Santa, flying that flimsy sleigh three thousand feet above the frozen earth. His pension fund has been raided, his Medicare reimbursements have been cut, and the doctor is recommending a triple bypass. That right jolly old elf is a basket case, grinning his worried chimpanzee grin, bravely ho ho ho-ing with so many skinny chimneys and needy children still before him.

Humor can be courage for the pregnant (young or old), courage for cops, ER nurses, and Afghan children, and courage for an old man flying into darkness. Laughter can be courage for anyone called to embark upon an unknown course along the bitter edge of life—which is to say, laughter can be a prelude to prayer and courage for us all.

THE MAGNIFICAT

My soul magnifies the Lord,
and my spirit rejoices in God my Savior
for He has looked with favor on the lowliness of His servant.
Surely from now on all generations will call me blessed,
for the Mighty One has done great things for me,
And holy is His name.
          Luke 1:46–49

"So, a dyslexic walks into a bra . . ."

PART THREE

Ask

13

Requests, Pleas, and Petitions

They went to a place called Gethsemane, and Jesus said to his disciples, "Sit here, while I pray."

He had with him Peter and James and John, and he began to be distressed and agitated. He said to them, "I am deeply grieved, even to death; Remain here, and keep awake."

And going a little farther, he threw himself on the ground and prayed that, if it were possible, the hour might pass from him. "Abba, Father, for you all things are possible; remove this cup from me . . ."

Mark 14:32–36

As a thirty-three-year-old widow, I had but one prayer: *Give him back to me.*

I prayed this very sincerely and very often. *For You, all things are possible. Give him back.*

"Two years ago," my cousin Ibbie told me, "my boyfriend asked me to go to Paris with him, and of course I was thrilled to go.

"Just before we left Seattle, I learned that a young math teacher at my children's school had been diagnosed with a very rare cancer of the bile duct and was not expected to live long—maybe a few weeks, with no treatment options.

"When we visited Montmartre in Paris, of course we went into Sacré-Coeur, and I was truly quite overwhelmed by how sacred the space felt. I felt as if I had walked into a place of God.

"My boyfriend, a physicist, was content to appreciate the architecture and then move on to the artists' square outside. I felt, however, that I needed to pray for a moment.

"I sat in a pew and felt tremendously focused and serious. I didn't think long—it just came to me to pray for the math teacher, who had a wife and three children. So I did.

"I thought about him and prayed for him and his family. I will never forget the darkness inside Sacré-Coeur, and the hundreds of candles that flickered hopefully, and the faces and souls of the believers and semibelievers and nonbelievers inside that space of God. I felt immersed and very, very serious."

Petitionary prayer is what we do when we pray for a fairly specific thing: that our airplane remains in the sky, that our children's math teacher be cured of bile duct cancer, that the people jumping in desperation from the windows of the World Trade Center will not be killed by the fall but will land lightly on their feet like the children in a Truffaut film. We pray that the hour of our death might pass and the poisoned cup be taken from us:

"With God, all things are possible," says Jesus.

Within the first week after Drew's accident, I received a note from the pastor of the Church of the Apostles down the street from my house. He wanted me to know that his congregation had prayed for my children and me. He didn't specify the content of the prayer, so for all I know, a whole congregation full of people who believed sincerely that with God, all things are possible were praying right along with me: *Please, please, please, just let him come back to life. Come on, God. Please.*

Petitionary prayer is the form of prayer that most obviously assumes a two-way communication between the supplicant and

God, but all prayer traditionally derives its value and its meaning from that assumption. "Hear my prayer, O Lord," the faithful sing.

William James—the nineteenth-century American pioneer in psychology and the psychology of religion, specifically—argued that petitionary prayer would be a problematic practice for Christianity in the modern age. He was the most articulate, if not the first, American to predict that as petitionary prayer was brought forward into a science-based world, it would be seen increasingly as inelegant and intellectually embarrassing, especially when placed alongside the marvels of science and scientific medicine.

Science historian (and professional skeptic) Dr. Michael Shermer has explained that even clever human beings are absurdly gullible when it comes to figuring out cause and effect. Petitionary prayer served well enough during the long, long period in our history during which solutions born of magical thinking (of one kind or another) were pretty much the only ones on tap anyway, and every proffered remedy came complete with supernatural explanations in case of failure. (Christians who would entreat God for relief from a painful illness knew to add, as Jesus did, "But not my will, but thine, be done.")

At least when it came to one's health, this was probably a good thing: As Shermer writes, "Medical historians . . . are in agreement that until well into the 20th century it was safer not to go to a doctor, thus leading to the success of such nonsense as homeopathy— a totally worthless nostrum that also did no harm, thus allowing the body to heal itself. Since humans are pattern-seeking animals we credit as the vector of healing whatever it was we did just before getting well."

A serious scientific examination of the claims made on prayer's behalf will yield results so inconsistent, they are just as plausibly explained by coincidence or chance. But let's imagine for a moment that petitionary prayer does "work" and that I (along with the kind churchgoers up the street) could pray to God and have God (for whom all things are possible) reconstruct my husband out of a jarful of cremains and restore him to the bosom of his family.

However deep my grief and fervent my desire for exactly this miracle, why should my importunings be met with divine generosity even as God is deaf to so many other, equally deserving petitioners? Millions have lost and will lose the ones they can't bear to be without. Many, perhaps most, of these mourners are also poor, oppressed, hungry, and frightened; why would I, a ridiculously fortunate American woman, be the sole widow whose loss God would prove willing to reverse? If I thought such a thing would actually happen, I hope I would be ashamed of myself for asking.

It won't happen, of course, but whenever and wherever a petitioner seems to receive just what he prays for, the theodicy problem tends to saunter back to center stage.

This is true not only of Christian prayer, of course. Some variant of this problem—why do bad things happen to good people; why are some spared and others lost? why aren't the innocent protected from the evil?—arises in any belief system in which the ultimate can be adjusted by the proximate, the eternal modified by those who, like leaves of grass, bloom for a season and then pass away.

We have quite a few such belief systems, but that probably says a lot more about the human ego than it does about the cosmos. The astonishingly popular book entitled *The Secret* provides a recent example.

Back in the day, the book jacket of *The Secret* would have been exactly what I would have wanted my personal book of prayers to look like: leathery, old, and worn, as if it might have been "accidentally" unearthed by goatherds from a tomb. The title is superimposed upon an image of a red wax seal. Way cool.

What is "the secret"? Well, it's called "The Law of Attraction." Basically, what you think becomes what you feel, and your feelings flow from your body as magnetic energy waves that travel over vast distances, somehow causing the universe around you to vibrate at exactly the same level of energy as your feelings. If your feelings are negative, the vibrations are going to produce negative experiences, but if you can think good thoughts and excrete good feelings, you'll have positive experiences. Like, say, a new and richer boyfriend or a Beemer.

It's true that you don't have a *conversation* with the universe when you want stuff—all that business about energy and vibrations makes it sound more scientific than your geezer-on-a-cloud religions. On the other hand, *The Secret* doesn't tell you to throw in even a soupçon of humility, none of that "not my will but yours" business, not even a "Please" or a "Thank You." Your will is identical with the will of the universe, or at least it shall be as soon as you get your mind in gear. Ask and ye shall receive, period.

To which the standard list of unmet human needs and undeserved and unsought human miseries can be offered as refutation: Auschwitz, the gulag, My Lai, Darfur . . . the East Asian tsunami, the earthquake in Haiti, famine in North Africa, floods in Bangladesh . . . hunger, malaria, drought, AIDS, multiple sclerosis, cancer . . .

Wait, but if you're talking about disease, the Secret Admirers have an answer: "Our physiology creates disease to give us feedback, to let us know we have an imbalanced perspective and we're not loving and we're not grateful," says F. Demartini in the DVD version of *The Secret*.

When she was an adolescent, my daughter Ellie had a friend whose family belonged to a Christian Science church. As long as they didn't talk about religion, Ellie and her friend got along fine. Problems arose, however, when the friend earnestly explained, "You don't need to take medicine for your eczema or your asthma. If you have faith and believe that the Divine Mind will heal you, they'll just go away."

She was trying to be helpful, Ellie assured me when describing this uncomfortable conversation. Ellie is a nicer person than I am and so was too tactful to inquire whether her friend's acne and inability to see without glasses were likewise evidence of inadequate faith and misguided belief.

Ellie was trying to avoid an interminable argument about illusion and reality, body and mind, health and faith. She was trying to receive what she knew to be an attempt at compassionate care.

What will cause the next bad thing that happens to me? It could be a nasty germ, the pesticides on an unwashed apple, a satanic neighbor, an incompetent doctor, or a rapist I am too weak to fight. Maybe it will have something to do with my pack-a-day habit or the heroin addiction I've been unable to kick. Maybe it will all come down to my ungrateful, unloving oh-ye-of-little-faith attitude. Whatever the cause of my suffering, I hope I will remember to look for God's works to be revealed in the love that surely will move other people to help, to pray, or to just sit down beside me and help me pass the time while the world has its way. I hope, too, that I will recognize these as miracles, as the purest sort of grace.

"Shortly after I got back to Seattle," my cousin told me, "I learned that the math teacher had recovered miraculously."

Now she prays every night when she walks her dogs under the stars and moon or beneath Seattle's normal overcast. She prays to be the kindest person she can be. She prays that the world finds its way toward better health. She prays for her children, her parents, and her extended family.

I don't know whether the math teacher's health was connected to my cousin's prayer with the same causal relationship that links Peter's blistered palate to the fact that he bit into the pizza before it cooled.

This I do know: The darkness, the candles, the beauty, and the silence called my cousin to attention, and attention sponsored love. The love encompassed not only her suffering friend but all those "believers, semibelievers, and nonbelievers" present with her on that day or throughout time. She knew herself to be numbered among the multitudes who had brought pain, hope, and thankfulness to the space that had been opened that God could enter and abide.

Maybe it was my cousin, immersed and serious within the Sacré-Coeur, who did the healing. Maybe it was the math teacher's medical care coupled with the strength his genes bestowed. Either way, his body's cells responded, and for now the math man lives.

My cousin told me she prays for her extended family. I'm part of that, so my cousin prays for me. I am happy not because her prayers appear to be effective but because I count it a privilege to be held in her heart.

I don't know precisely what words my cousin uses, nor do I know what the good people of the Church of the Apostles said when they prayed for me after my first husband died. The pastor did not volunteer this information, and I did not inquire. Instead, moved by their goodness and glad of their prayers, I cried, "How nice of you! Thank you!"

"You're welcome," the pastor said.

"May I pray for you, too?" I asked him eagerly, and he paused for a moment. Then, by grace, he answered:

"Yes. Thank you."

14

Finding the Right Words

I am not yet so sated, so jam-packed and blasé, that I can know-ingly turn down any kindness that comes my way. If someone is praying for me, I am touched no matter what words are used.

Still, when it came to establishing my own spiritual routine, a significant delay was caused by my unwillingness to use words someone else had come up with. *Surely,* I thought, back when I was first gettin' religion, *I can come up with my own words for this odd, disquieting, and compelling experience: I'm a writer, for God's sake!*

"Are you?" said God. (She sounded interested but unconvinced.)

I went out and purchased a blank book.

Blank books are irresistible. I had a lot of them around already, waiting to be used, but the book in which I would write my prayers should, I thought, have a certain spiritual look to it.

A brownish faux-ancient cover would give it an air of serious-ness of purpose. I wanted Florentine endpapers and handmade pages, too, but then I remembered that handmade paper tends to be soft, and the ink would bleed. I didn't want my prayers to look all mushy, which meant I would need to use a Sharpie. But a Sharpie would make my prayers smell industrial, and when it came to scent, I was thinking more along the lines of myrrh or maybe patchouli.

"First clean the inside of the cup," Jesus advises. "Then worry about what the outside looks like; Whitewashing a sepulcher won't alter what's within."

Gold leaf! I thought. Hasn't gold always been used to add a little pizzazz to the sacred? ("Actually, it's the other way around," mumbled Jesus.)

Clearly, I thought that the biggest difficulty about spiritual writing was finding the right container. If I could just find a book that looked like the handmade product of a fourth-century monastery, excellent prayers worthy of the borrowed luster of antiquity would flow forth from my pen. Both the seeker and the huckster know that when it comes to religion, antiquity equals authority.

"Why not use the old prayers, then?" asked Jesus.

"Because the whole point is to correct the defects of the old prayers!" I declared. "Don't worry, Jesus. I'm going to create just the sort of prayers that would have been written in the first place if only those ancients had been as educated and clever as I am."

Predictably, nice blank book or no nice blank book, my prayers were dismal failures—puny, stingy bits of nonsense by a young person so fearful of saying something irrational or politically incorrect that she couldn't say anything. "Straining out gnats, swallowing camels," said Jesus dolefully. "Again."

No problem. With the flexibility of youth, I decided that since my prayers were hypocritical, lawless, self-indulgent crap, prayer itself must be foolish and unnecessary. "I, by my works, will show you my faith!" I snapped triumphantly in Jesus' direction, thus unwittingly placing an obstacle in my own spiritual path that would hamper my progress for the next several years.

Writers, preachers, and theologians, especially those in the Protestant tradition, really love words, and the authors of the Bible fell into all three categories. It is no wonder that the Gospel of John confidently proclaims that *in the beginning was the Word.*

As it happens, I fall into all three categories as well, so you will not be surprised to find prayer taking the form of words here. Still, prayer becomes prayer not just because the best, most perfect words are written or spoken. Instead, there is a kind of alchemy in which words are made gold through their relationship with all that cannot be written or spoken: arbitrary chance and chancy history, and the memory of all the human voices that have joined in this same utterance often enough and deliberately enough that the words have shed their meaning and become rhythms, notes, sonic links to a common ancestry, whether of blood or of belief.

All this is in place and influencing the experience of a prayer before you or I open our mouth and form the first syllable. Which isn't to say that you shouldn't write your own prayers, nor that you mustn't buy or create books or other beautiful accoutrements, only that you don't *have* to.

While the creation of beauty (including beautiful words) has an important place in any religion's exploration and expression, it is always potentially hazardous to the enterprise as a whole. For any people and in every epoch there arises the confusion between looking good and being good. You and I happen to live during a period when this confusion feeds and is fed by an extraordinary hyperconsumption of material things from all over the world. A marvelous but extremely intrusive mass media relentlessly encourages us to respond to every impulse with a shopping spree, translating even our deepest values into a reason to purchase. (When I resolve—or rather, re-resolve—to start exercising regularly, my first impulse is not to drop to the floor and do some push-ups. Instead, I'll spend an hour online-shopping for a new sports bra.)

Commerce too often extracts its living through the assiduous cultivation of two chronic human weaknesses: anxiety and self-indulgence. Since we pray to *reduce* anxiety and to *counter* self-indulgence (among other reasons), it makes a lot more sense to begin a life of prayer by saying the prayers you already know (your remembered childhood grace or bedtime blessing) and hold off on the fancy bits and bobs until you've had time to develop your own sense of the words or material objects that serve your practice.

If I may say so, you might want to be particularly cautious when it comes to unfamiliar spiritual or religious traditions.

There have been American Buddhists as long as people have immigrated here from Asia, but in the last fifty years or so, Buddhism has gained rapidly in popularity and is developing American versions of its various forms—among them Theravada, Mahayana, Pure Land, and Zen. Buddhist ideas, naturally enough, have affected the evolution of other traditions as well.

Thus, I've had a self-described fundamentalist Christian tell me in all sincerity that after her death, she fully expected to be reincarnated as a dolphin. This from a salt-of-the-earth Baptist in rural Maine!

There is an endearing open-mindedness and optimism in the American spirit, which is healthy, generally speaking. Is it any wonder that the children of these rural Mainers are having images of the Buddha tattooed on their shoulder blades along with the Hindi Om, the yin-yang, and maybe a pentagram for good measure?

I'm puritanical about tattoos, so my children were forbidden from getting tattoos at least as long as they remained under my roof and were covered by my health insurance (don't ask me why the insurance was part of the rule: I blurted it out and then had to stick by it). However, I advised, should any of them choose to get inked as adults, they should thoroughly explore the traditional significance of any symbol they found appealing before giving it permanent skin room. It is easy to imagine that you fully grasp a concept like karma, for example, and have only the faintest sense of its meaning. Moreover, symbols that strike the uninitiated as merely attractive or vaguely spiritual are likely to be taken quite seriously by others. Even the most lackadaisical Muslim or Hindu might consider it disrespectful to find ALLAH AKBAR or OM tattooed across my child's bicep (to say nothing of the effect it would have as a tramp stamp).

"Yes, Peter," I said when he challenged me. "You have the right to free speech—that is, you will have it once you're an adult and no longer on my health insurance. I'm just suggesting that you are going to want to choose your words carefully, especially if you're going to have them written permanently on your body. Good, bad, or meaningless, there it will be: bunchy with fat or sagging from the bone, fading, freckling, wrinkling, and drooping so long as flesh endures."

You can't count on manufacturers to do the research for you, either. In 1985 French perfumier Jean-Paul Guerlain (hardly an unsophisticated hack) created an "Asian-influenced" perfume that the company called Samsara.

It's a pleasing word in an English speaker's ear, mildly melodic, agreeably sibilant. The business legend claims it was inspired by Guerlain's romance with a pretty but apparently not Buddhist maiden. Had she been Buddhist, she might have informed her fragrant beau that "Samsara" is the Sanskrit word for the realm of struggle, pain, anxiety, and hatred, the very world that Hindus and Buddhists are doing their best to get out of.

Evidently, no Guerlain executive then or since thought to page through a copy of *Sanskrit for Dummies* before using a Sanskrit word. If they did, they cynically (and, for the most part, correctly) assumed that the rest of us wouldn't know the difference. Out came the "spiritual" advertising, including a television commercial in which an extremely well-groomed (Caucasian) fashion model gazes at a lotus blossom with rapt serenity while the sound track whispers, "Samsara . . . Samsara . . . Samsara . . ."

Ignorance is an issue not only for dabblers in non-Christian traditions. "When I become a Christian," writes R. C. Sproul, a conservative theologian, in *Now, That's a Good Question!* "my heart changes immediately . . . but God doesn't drill a hole in my head and fill it with new information and teach me overnight all the things that he wants me to know about who he is and what he wants me to do . . . the metaphor that the Bible uses is the distinction between meat and milk. He calls us first to begin with milk . . . and then to move on to the heavier matters—to the meat. My big concern is that it seems that we are on a diet of milk and are terrified to eat anything more substantial."

"Terrified" might be the right word: Commerce cherry-picks

world religions, including Christianity, for the pretty images and nice words and ignores the scary, ugly, challenging parts.

Take Psalm 137, for example: *By the rivers of Babylon—there we sat down and there we wept when we remembered Zion.*

Bob Marley sings a memorable reggae version, but he sticks to the first verses. If you hear this psalm in church, the chances are very good that the reader will do the same thing, tactfully leaving the last two verses unread: *O daughter Babylon, you devastator! Happy shall they be who pay you back what you have done to us! Happy shall they be who take your little ones and dash them against the rock!*

I suppose there exists a passionately Christian teenager who could be moved to have these words (or an image of someone dashing babies against stones) tattooed on his chest. If so, I don't want that guy dating my daughter.

While we're on the subject of Bible verses, may I remind you of something obvious: that the Bible is really, really old? Perhaps that sounds dismissive. If so, that isn't my intention. But one of the problems with words that were written down long, long ago is that words and phrases occur and are transmitted within the context of the surrounding culture. They do not exist in pure isolation, independent of the people who wrote or spoke them. When I say something in English to another American, we are using words that not only signify specific things but convey additional, usually unspoken meanings based on common cultural references.

I demonstrated this to a roomful of people once by saying the words "plop plop, fizz fizz."

"What comes next?" I asked.

"Oh, what a relief it is" came the answer, but not from the entire crowd. Those under the age of thirty-five or who had been born or brought up overseas responded with confused silence. For those who had grown up in the United States during the sixties and early seventies and had owned a television or radio, I had said the first line of a familiar jingle from an advertisement for Alka-Seltzer.

It might have been easily thirty years since the advertisement was last played over the airwaves, and yet the older people could complete the rhyme and hum the familiar tune together.

If I were to give a sermon to this latter group, and I wanted to make a passing reference to the idea of blessed relief from acute discomfort, I could throw in the phrase "plop plop fizz fizz." Without explaining or even finishing the rhyme, I could evoke this and all sorts of other ideas and impressions—American eating habits, upset stomachs, the ubiquity of advertising in the modern age, and the astonishing staying power of the commercial jingle—but it would work only if my audience shared that referent.

To my own children—let alone a person happening upon my sermons a thousand years from now—those four words could convey nothing at all.

"Plop plop fizz fizz" was a tidbit of American culture that was transmitted orally and aurally rather than in writing. Most languages, throughout most of history, were and remain oral languages. While English has a "standard" written form, it also has many variants, and most of these remain primarily oral languages. All language is subject to a phenomenon linguists call "semantic drift," which happens more rapidly and is more noticeable in oral language and slang. A couple of generations is enough to make for confusion.

Take the memorable luncheon my children and I were treated to by Great-aunt Harriet and her husband, Great-uncle Walter. I had noticed, not long before this excursion, an increasing tendency among my young to indulge in scatological or otherwise inappropriate discussions at mealtime. Hoping to spare the Great Ones the shock of hearing what cometh from the mouths of babes, I spoke firmly to the babes before we joined our relatives about the need for good manners and polite conversation.

At the table, Great-aunt Harriet ordered her usual cocktail (a Bloody Mary—pale pink, no vegetables, produced according to her own recipe) while the children received Shirley Temples. Great-uncle Walter and I had iced tea. The children were behaving admirably. Upon request, Ellie demonstrated her ability to spell

difficult words like "rhythm" and "chagrin"; Woolie showed everyone the gap in her gums where her molar had been; and Zach and
Peter politely listened to Great-uncle Walter reminisce about his
days as manager of a Necco Wafer factory. I began to relax.

Then came one of those silent spaces that open up in a conversation, just long enough to make the next phrase sound out loud
and clear.

"Well, you know, Ellie," Great-aunt Harriet was saying, "your
Great-uncle Walter was not the first man to make love to me."

Instantly, the attention of everyone at the table (and everyone at
the surrounding tables) was riveted.

"He wasn't?" Ellie asked.

"Oh, no! I was popular, my dear! There were many young fellows who thought I was awfully attractive, weren't there, Walter?"

"I suppose," mumbled Great-uncle Walter uncertainly.

"That dear Phillip Chase . . . you remember Phillip, don't you?"

"Oh . . . oh, yes," said Great-uncle Walter. "Went into banking,
didn't he?"

"It was right at the start of the war. He was older than I was, old
enough to enlist, and he used to come visit me in his uniform. So
dashing!" Great-aunt Harriet tittered reminiscently.

"War?" asked Peter with interest.

"Which war?" Zach was obviously picturing John Wayne or
maybe Charlton Heston.

"And there we would be, he and I, on the couch before the
fire . . . so romantic, don't you think? Phillip would make love to
me all afternoon . . ."

"Oh!" said Ellie, turning to Great-uncle Walter, her face puck-
ered with compassion. She put her hand on his arm. "Didn't you
mind?"

"Phillip was good at lovemaking," Great-aunt Harriet declared
judiciously. "Better than Walter, really. When there were several
fellows visiting at the same time, you could tell the difference."

"I'll bet Great-uncle Walter was plenty good at . . . you know,"
said Peter with pugnacious loyalty, while Zach guffawed into his

napkin and Woolie gazed about with her usual air of disingenuous innocence singing, "Making love in the afternoon . . . making love in the afternoon" under her breath.

Leaping up, I announced that it was time for all the children to wash their hands.

"I already washed my—"

"Come along!" In the corridor outside the restrooms, I told them that in the olden days, back in the 1940s, the term "making love" did not refer to sexual intercourse but to flirting and maybe cuddling. "It's called semantic drift," I explained, and gave them a short lecture on linguistics, if only to distract them from the disturbing image of Great-aunt Harriet gettin' jiggy with Charlton and John.

If a mere half century can transform innocent flirtation into an orgy on a hearthrug, imagine what two thousand years can do.

That the Bible itself is a dominant common reference in Western discourse makes this even more interesting. "That mother thinks her kid walks on water," the harassed teacher of a spoiled child might complain, while in Holland, young people who find entertainment in deliberately drinking themselves into a stupor will refer to this as getting "Lazarus drunk," meaning, of course, that they shall have to be raised from the dead. In time, a phrase like "walks on water" can acquire the meaning of "perfect" without the speaker even knowing that he or she is referring to a story in the Bible about Jesus.

"Plop plop fizz fizz." Jesus could keep his sermons short because he could count on his words carrying both their obvious meaning and their hidden referential power. *My God, why hast thou forsaken me?* is a line his Jewish hearers would easily recognize as the first words of Psalm 22, one that carries some of the most heartrending descriptions of human misery ever written (*I am poured out like water, and all my bones are out of joint; my heart is like wax; it is melted within my breast . . . dogs are all around me*) and also a description of the ultimate triumph of God over "all the families of the nations." If we know nothing more than the evident source, there's plenty of culturally dependent meaning packed into that one line. For all we know, the fullest, richest meaning of the psalm—and thus the line—requires the reader to have the same cultural background as the psalmist. Though biblical historians try hard to paint a detailed picture of the first century for us, it would have to be impossibly fine-grained to give us the generational nuances of a phrase as fungible as "making love," let alone the alterations that semantic drift might bring to a phrase like "in the beginning was the Word."

Every religion—every single one—has problematic passages in its scripture or repellent notions lurking somewhere in its ethos. Some may be incomprehensible, as if the semantics have drifted beyond our ken; but the deeper we go into Jewish, Buddhist, Hindu, even humanist history, literature, and practice, the more apt we are to come across thinkers and thoughts that seem so unjust, arrogant, or unloving that they verge on the diabolical. (Margaret Sanger, pioneer in birth control and 1957 Humanist of the Year, was a firm believer in the sterilization and segregation of the unfit, for example.) When faced with this problem, the obvious conclusion— certainly the conclusion I was drawn to for many years—is that all established religions are hopelessly corrupt, and we'll have to start all over again from our smarter and more knowledgeable perspective. However, most—perhaps all—religions were founded by people who thought that was exactly what they were doing, which should give even the most confident would-be modern messiah pause.

As is probably obvious by now, I've given up expecting to find a perfect faith. Or perhaps it's that the perfect faith can be revealed only in and through an ongoing conversation between faiths— "Faiths" with a capital F (Islam, Buddhism, Judaism, Catholicism), and the small-F faith each of us carries around.

EXPECT IMPURITY! my religious bumper sticker would proclaim. Doubt, frustration, and plain hard work are inevitable and more or less permanent features of a spiritual life. How could it be otherwise? No word, book, story, scent, or pretty statue can mask for long the essential pathos of the human being struggling to extract transcendent meaning from her merely human life.

Who listens to our words when we pray? Perhaps no one.
Will our prayers be answered? Probably not.
Then what the hell are we supposed to do?
Pray.
Alleluia!
Amen.

15

Avoiding the Wrong Words

"If you believe in prayer, don't curse. A curse is a prayer."
Sergeant Stephen Tuel,
Frederick Police Department,
Maryland

The Lord is my shepherd, I shall not want. When I say these words
at a memorial service or funeral, most of the congregation will join
with me for the rest of the psalm, at least if most happen to have
been born or raised Jewish or Christian. Even if they are too polite
or shy to do so aloud, I can see folks following along silently, their
lips moving, the phrases familiar.

The words "memorial," "memorize," and "membership" are all
etymologically linked: To memorialize is to remember, and to
remember is to recall one's own or another's membership within a
human community.

Those of us who grew up in a time or place in which what was
old, let alone ancient, seemed inherently suspect may resist mem-
orizing prayers like this one, pointing out—with considerable
justice—that the language is exclusively masculine, hierarchical,
undemocratic, and comes from a book only Jews and Christians
think of as sacred. Reciting the Twenty-third Psalm, therefore,
affirms the "membership" of only some, not all.

Moreover, reliance on traditional language raises other issues. While much of the comfort and community of church life were denied me as a child, at least I was never subjected to the punitive, damaging effects that religious imagery and language can have when they come from the mouth of an abusive person.

So while I may have objected, quite strenuously at times, to the various iniquities of traditional religious word and praxis, mine were essentially brain-based objections. My heart does not contract in reflexive terror at the sight of a clerical collar, and I do not taste the tinny flavor of remembered shame whenever anyone mentions God, God's judgment, or God's forgiveness.

I can read, study, discuss, and reason my way through any problems I might have with religious language, and on the basis of what I learn, I can either accept or reject it. A professor at seminary can offer me a new way of looking at a biblical text, and within an hour, that text can go from profane to sacred in my eyes.

But if you have been on the receiving end of abuse in a religious context, you can't think your way out of it. Trauma lodges in the body, and if it gets the chance to put down roots, it may never be fully expunged, no matter how strenuously someone tries to argue it away. If you have been insulted, humiliated, or sexually assaulted by someone in a clerical collar, the clerical collar I wear around my neck may never again signal kindness and care to you. (This is one of the reasons I wear a Roman collar: It is swiftly and easily removed.)

Once I was asked to marry a couple who had grown up in different religious traditions. The groom had been raised Catholic, and while he no longer went to Mass and may even, he admitted, have become an atheist, he had no particular animus against the Church and was happy to have traditional Christian language used in his wedding ceremony.

The bride, on the other hand, had been raised in the southern United States in a reformed tradition, where she had learned the Lord's Prayer in a context she experienced as self-righteous, racist, sexist, angry, and, frankly, frightening.

She knew that her family would expect the Lord's Prayer to be spoken at any "real" wedding, and she wanted to accommodate them. (It was enough of a stretch for them, she told me, that the presiding minister would be a woman!) Still, though it made her feel silly to admit it, the Lord's Prayer gave her the willies.

It did no good to point out that the Lord's Prayer is a very nice, unobjectionable prayer, that it isn't intrinsically violent or racist or even particularly Christian, insofar as it never mentions Christ. The bride couldn't hear the Lord's Prayer without blanching, and we didn't want the bride to blanch on her wedding day.

The solution we came up with ended up being the coolest part of the service. I said the Lord's Prayer—but I said it in Koine Greek. In introducing this novelty to the congregation, I pointed out that Koine Greek was the language in which the prayer was first written down (Matthew 6:9–13 and Luke 11:2–4). Indeed, it was quite possibly the language Jesus used when he first said it aloud to his disciples, since this "low," or everyday, "coin of the realm" dialect was the language all inhabitants of the Holy Land would be sure to have in common.

The bride's folks were charmed to hear the words as Jesus might have said them; the groom's mother felicitously recalled some Greek ancestors; and though "Our father who art in heaven" made the bride tense and miserable, *Pater hemon, ho en tois ouranois* went down a treat.

When reading the Twenty-third Psalm at my grandmother's funeral, my aunt Ellen deviated from the version familiar to most of the family in order to honor her mother, who had emigrated from Denmark to America in the 1930s.

> Skal jeg end vandre I Dødsskyggens Dal
> Jeg frygter ej ondt; this due r med mig,
> Din koep og din Stave r min Trøst.

The rest of us didn't understand a word she was saying, but it was a beautiful, genuine prayer.

On Mother's Day, I will often invite a congregation to join me in the Lord's Prayer with only a single word changed:

Our mother who art in heaven
Hallowed be thy name
Thy kingdom come . . .

I don't do this with the intention of declaring that God is—or ought to be—female. I suppose I could ask the congregation to question their own assumptions about the gender of God and what that means about the gender of power and responsibility in the world, but that isn't my agenda, at least not in the pulpit on Mother's Day. I just like the way that one small change can open up the prayer and let me hear it in a new way.

My husband, Simon, loyally seated in a pew on Mother's Day, told me afterward that when he prayed this, the *Mater Nostra,* and came to the line "give us this day our daily bread," he had a clear image for the first time in a lifetime of saying that prayer of someone holding out bread to him.

"How did you respond?" I asked.

"I said thank you," said Simon.

There is nothing disingenuous or sacrilegious about changing the words of a prayer: The Bible itself contains different versions for many stories and prayers, and God is named and described in many, many ways. This is obvious enough even before we get into all the languages into which the Bible has been translated, let alone all the other world scriptures that have named the sacred in yet more ways, with yet more metaphors.

In the Bible, God is Yahweh, Adonai, "the one who sees," and "the one who hears my voice." He is a mother hen, Jesus' daddy, a mighty fortress, and a still, small voice.

In order to speak of God at all, we have to use some sort of word, but to insist on the perfection of a particular word is to mistake the window for the view.

If it helps to play around with the words, do it. Take advantage of the extraordinary media diversity of our time and find prayers that cover the same spiritual territory without aggravating the injuries that you neither inflicted on yourself nor deserved. If you need to, you can write your own prayers: The plainest envelope-and-ballpoint-pen prayer you give to yourself will carry you closer to God than the classic that makes you sick to your stomach. This was a ballpoint-pen-and-envelope prayer:

May love and strength be in my hands
May love and courage be in my heart
May love and wisdom be in my mind
May love be with me and work through me today
And in all my days.
Amen.
    KB

This one was, too:

May God bless and protect me
May God smile on me and smile through me
May God befriend me and let me be a better friend
May God make me peaceful and a maker of peace.
Amen.
    KB

I am able to pray using a name that was known to my forebears as it will doubtless be known to my descendants: the name of God. This name, and my willingness to say it, are accidents of history: the history of our language, the history of English-speaking people, my personal history that left that word essentially untarnished.

But prayer, like the Sabbath, was made for the human, not the human for the prayer. If you can't use the word "God," don't use it. If you were abused or violated by someone who cloaked his evil beneath a mantle of faith, you have as much right to all the gifts of the human spiritual tradition as anyone else, and far more right to it than your abuser does.

Reject certain prayers or all prayer, certain churches or all houses of worship. Go ahead and toss the whole religious kit and caboodle overboard if you genuinely have no need of it. But don't let the lies and violence of predators, the purveyors of bigotry, and thieves of faith take this gift of prayer from you, too. These are your human birthright: a consciousness capable of increase, an empathy inclined to expand. They belong to you, for you are a child of God.

You are my shepherd
I shall not want
You cradle me in green pastures
You lead me beside the still waters
You return my soul to me.
You guide me in the paths of righteousness
For You are righteous
Though I walk through the valley of the shadow of death, I fear
        no evil, for You are with me;
Your rod and your staff comfort me
You spread a table before me in the presence of my enemies
You soothe my head with oil
My cup runs over
Surely goodness and mercy will follow me all the days of my life
And I will dwell in Your house forever.

16

Prayer for
Atheists and Agnostics

Did you hear about the dyslexic, agnostic insomniac?
She lay awake all night, wondering: "Does Dog exist?"

In my youth, I was agnostic. Then I decided I'd go for broke and be
an atheist. Later on, when I realized that neither of the A-words fit,
I still tried to avoid using the word "God." It carries so much patriarchal baggage, and the feminist alternative, "Goddess," sounds too
much like "stewardess" or "actress," a demeaning diminutive of a
"real" word that was reserved for men.

Besides, I thought I had invented this brand-new Thing, this
Spirit, this . . . Well, George Lucas had taken the word "Force," or I
would have given that a try. "May the Force be with you" could be
a really cool blessing if only Obi-Wan Kenobi hadn't said it first.

Anyway, here was this Thing I was called to serve and worship,
but naturally, there would be no irrationalities or bigotries in my
practice! And since my conception of the Holy was shiny-new and
pure, why name it by that old, discredited three-letter word?

C. S. Lewis evidently went through a phase in which he insisted
on calling God Yahweh, which is how one pronounces the Hebrew
tetragrammaton YHWH, by which the Ineffable is indicated but

not actually entitled. Because God cannot be contained within any human mind, let alone pegged into place by a human word, YHWH is an indicator rather than a name.

Anyway, Lewis went around Oxford calling God Yahweh and explaining to anyone who asked (and quite a few who didn't) why we should all be saying Yahweh and calling ourselves Yahwists. At last he realized that he was becoming insufferable (I suspect wedgies or swirlies might have been involved), and he went back to using comprehensible, communicative language.

I like C. S. Lewis for the same reason that I used to despise him: because he's such a know-it-all. It is his weakness and his strength.

Because I came back to God (the word and the Word) by a route that Lewis might have recognized, saying "God" out loud always gives me a bracing little jolt of humility. Until I no longer feel that jolt, I shall have to assume I've still got ego moles to be whacked, although I am glad to report that the moles, like their whacker, seem to be slowing down with age. They pop their grizzled heads up a little less often and with a tad less vigor than they once did.

To reject not words but the Word is to distance myself from all the human beings who have tried to pray that word, to open their minds wider and love more. It is to presume that I am smarter than all of them and less needy. I can't even fake that presumption anymore.

Try this game with your loved ones:

Q. If you were a domestic animal, what kind of domestic animal would you be?
A. _____
Q. Why?
A. Because _____s are _____ and _____.
Q. Okay, if you were a wild animal, what kind would you be?
A. _____
Q. Why?
A. _____

The domestic animal represents the way you think other people see you. The wild animal is how you see yourself.

If you're interested, my domestic animal was a dog (friendly, loving), and my wild animal was . . . no, not a mole! A dolphin (cheerful, smart, creative).

I played this game with a large, loud, intimidating state police lieutenant. Dennis Hayden's domestic animal was a dog. Why?

"Because they're friendly," Dennis said. "And they get to lie around and take naps."

His wild animal was a lion, because everyone is afraid of lions, but as he wistfully pointed out, all they really do is lie around and take naps.

Okay, a simple, silly game can reveal a general theme in a person's character—and this can be entertaining or even mildly illuminating. I'll give you another game to play, which I recommend especially if your problem with the word "God" is that it evokes only an image of that cranky Caucasian senior citizen lounging on a cloud, occasionally bestirring himself to hurl a lightning bolt at some unsuspecting sinner. It is definitely difficult to pray to such an unhelpful deity as this.

So, okay: What sort of Dog *could* you pray to?

Before you answer ("Beagle!"), try this:

Fill in the blank:

Nothing matters more than _____.

When you have filled in the blank, you will have given yourself a functional definition of God.

I believe absolutely, implacably, irretrievably, and indefatigably that nothing matters more than love. I believe all human souls are called to become as loving as they possibly can be, given the limitations that time and luck will inevitably impose. Love is the point, the purpose, and the ultimate value; it is consciousness and empathy, alpha and omega, beginning and end. *God is love.*

While there is surely a downside to having such an embarrassingly simple theology, the upside is that my beliefs do not include the necessity of converting others to my view. However convinced I might be that you and I are both called to love God (which is to say, to love Love) and to love each other and to help each other become more loving, it isn't a problem if your view differs. I love you anyway. (So there.)

The other advantage is that I have a handy single-syllable synonym that can be used interchangeably with the word "God" (at least in English). Love can thus be substituted (with perhaps a little additional tweaking but no real offense to orthodoxy) into any traditional prayer. To wit:

O love that is of heaven
Hallowed be the name of love
May love's dominion come
The will of love be done
On earth as it must be in any heaven worthy of the name.

May love give us this day our daily bread
May love forgive our trespasses as we forgive those who trespass
  against us.

May love lead us not into temptation, but deliver us from evil;
For the Kingdom, the power, and the glory belong to love
Forever and ever.
Amen.
  KB

PART FOUR

❧

Celebrate

17

Singing Your Prayers

Today, like every day
We wake up hollow and frightened.
Don't open the door to the study and begin reading.
Reach for a musical instrument.
Let the beauty we love be what we do
There are hundreds of ways to kneel and kiss the ground.
                    Jalal al-Din Rumi

One year, around the holidays, the Sunday-school teacher at our church decided to have all the kids sing a song as part of the Christmas Eve service. She chose a round to be sung in simple Latin and told everybody to practice it often at home. My kids spent the weeks leading up to Christmas marching around the house, belting out *"Gaudeamus Hodie!"* Which would have been very sweet, except that they thought the words were "Goddamn! A moose!"

Q. Why do Unitarian Universalists sing so badly?
A. They're too busy reading ahead in the hymnal to make
   sure they agree with the lyrics.

There are many things I would be unwilling to speak but am nonetheless happy to sing. Maybe this is because the words in a song are rhythmic elements at least as much as they are words, and the voices are musical instruments rather than speech machines. Oh, I would draw the line at the "Horst Wessel Song," but I'm happy to sing all sorts of hymns ("The Old Rugged Cross," "O Christ Jesus Sent from Heaven") whose lyrics, were they to be put forth as statements, would provoke me to debate or at least to ask for nuance. This is even truer of Christmas carols, blissfully sung in defiance of any doctrine I might hold firm.

Fall on your knees . . . O hear the angel voices . . . The choir up front, in their once-a-year robes, their earnest eyebrows flying upward in unison on the high notes, and the packed pews giving forth the sacred sound—rumbly, squeaky—of a congregation joined. *O night divine . . .*

A Jesuit priest, Father Greg Boyle, who works in Los Angeles with juvenile offenders and gang members, has said that his favorite Christmas carol is "O Holy Night," because it contains these lines:

> *Long lay the world in sin and error pining*
> *Till He appeared and the soul felt its worth.*

"And the soul felt its worth," Father Boyle repeated, and wondered aloud whether any of us might, like Christ, somehow be able to offer our neighbor such love that her soul feels its worth. Maybe our faces should serve as loving mirrors, capable of revealing to a neighbor how good and beautiful she really is.

Ever since hearing Father Boyle speak on the radio, I have considered "O Holy Night" to be a prayer.

Do you need scriptural justification for singing as prayer? The Psalms were originally songs—the word "psalm" means "song, sung to a harp" in Greek—so there is no reason why a prayer cannot be sung, or a song cannot be a prayer. It doesn't even have to be an explicitly "religious" song.

Sometimes it's better if the song is not explicitly religious.

Periodically, dear friends do their best to interest me in Christian music, and I do try. Sometimes, here or there, I'll like a song and even get a glimpse of why it might be so deeply meaningful to the person who shared it with me. Usually, however, I find the lyrics a little too obviously scriptural, a little too explicit in their statements of dogma, and the music isn't quite interesting enough to counter it. Ironically, I think, the lyrics written by a self-consciously Christian musician might suffer from the same problem I had when trying to write my own prayers: I was so determined not to say the wrong thing that my prayers offered no room to breathe, no open ends or open questions, so they conveyed nothing that felt deeply, inexpressibly right.

I can pray "O Holy Night" not because its words match my particular dogma line for line but because the words and melody hold and release so much for me: memory, history, the heat, scent, and sound of those singing in the pew beside me, Father Boyle's remarks and his redemptive work with overlooked and wasted children (how could anyone overlook and waste a child?), the warmth of the church and the cold outside. With all of this, the song demands, "Fall on your knees. Hear the angel voices . . ."

And I answer: *Yes.*

And: *Thank you.*

Choosing the first hymn for the service I had been invited to conduct on the Sunday after September 11 was easy. I, like thousands of other ministers across the country, wrote "America the Beautiful" onto the list that I was preparing for the music director, and I immediately began to cry.

O beautiful for patriot dream
That sees beyond the years
Thine alabaster cities gleam
Undimmed by human tears . . .

The congregation managed—barely—to warble their way through the hymn, and if it wasn't the best singing they had ever done, it was one of the most heartfelt prayers I've ever heard.

Remember the scene in *Casablanca* when the Nazis arrive in Sam's bar to announce that the Germans have defeated the French, and therefore all French colonies belong to Germany? The French customers begin to sing "L'Hymne National Français," La Marseillaise.

> *Allons enfants de la Patrie,*
> *Le jour de gloire est arrivé!*

Whatever it means ("Come, children of the homeland, the day of glory has arrived!"), that moment in the movie brings a lump to my throat, even though I'm not French. I think it is because I recognize it as a prayer.

I'm fond of my own country's *hymne national,* although I admit to being among those who can't hit the high notes ("and the rocket's red gla-aare!") without standing on my toes, and sometimes not even then. Still, what I love is that this song—our national anthem—isn't triumphalist or even particularly martial, though the poem was written after and about a battle. It doesn't wind itself up with a great blare of trumpets, a crash of drums, and the conclusion that we're number one! It concludes with a question:

> O say, does that star-spangled banner yet wave
> O'er the land of the free and the home of the brave?

Every time we sing it, before ball games and graduations, at the inauguration of a president or a celebration for our new citizens, we ask that question of one another and implicitly acknowledge the best thing about America.

What distinguishes us from every other country on earth is that America began and remains an extraordinary and courageous experiment in human freedom. While wealth and power are agreeable things for a nation to have, they are not what defines us. Nor are we defined by the landscape—however beautiful—or by a shared history, shared skin color, or even the shared language of our citizens.

An American is a human being willing to participate in the experiment, willing to agree and believe "that all men [and women] are created equal, that they are endowed by their Creator with certain unalienable Rights, that among these are Life, Liberty and the pursuit of Happiness."

This America is a rare, delicate, and precious thing. Our anthem sensibly asks us to check, every time we mumble, warble, and shriek our way through it: Look around you, friends. Can you see if the Star-spangled Banner is still waving over a land that continues to belong to the free, a land that remains the home of the brave?

By grace, may we always be able to answer with the simplest prayer of the Desert Fathers (and my mother-in-law): *Yes.* And *Thank you.*

18

Speechless Prayers

Pray without ceasing, Saint Francis of Assisi advised. "If necessary, use words." Through my artist husband, I have become acquainted with the work of Brother Thomas, a Benedictine monk and ceramicist. During his inarguably well-spent life (he died in August 2007 at the age of seventy-eight), he wrote much and well about clay, creativity, love, and prayer. "When we encounter the Holy, words fail," he has written.

If you think about it, that's a strange point for a Christian to make, given the statement "In the beginning was the Word." Brother John was qualified to make it, given that he was one of those gifted souls capable not only of making beautiful art but of writing beautiful words.

Last May, the colonel of the Maine Warden Service offered me a choice. Did I want to come to the annual law-enforcement memorial ceremony in Augusta as a chaplain—or as a survivor? Silly question: I wanted to come as a chaplain! (Being a survivor hurts.)

I came in my uniform, and I sat next to the colonel, and I was fine until they said my late husband's name (James Andrew Griffith). Then lo and behold (and unfortunately without a Kleenex handy), it turned out I am a survivor after all.

* * *

In October 2001 (a month, that is, after 9/11), I met a friend, a retired detective from the city of New York, when he came to Maine to do some training with the Community Policing Institute. My friend seemed awfully tired; he had spent the past few weeks with other active and retired NYPD detectives sifting through the debris and dust from the World Trade Center, looking for material, including human remains, that might identify a victim still unaccounted for.

The work, conducted at Fresh Kills landfill on Staten Island, was physically taxing, hazardous to health, and heartbreaking. My detective friend had been present on the day a front-end loader emptied a half ton of debris and someone caught a glint of silver. There, amid the dust and ash, was a patrolman's badge.

It still made him cry to think about it.

When I got home from the training, I told Zachary about the work on Staten Island, the detectives, and the badge in the ashes.

"Oh, Mom," Zach said. "I wish I could do something for those guys."

"Me, too."

"If Dad was alive, he would go help them."

"Yes," I agreed.

Zach thought about it for a moment. Then he said, "We will send them Dad's flag."

I knew which flag he meant. It was the flag that had been draped over his father's coffin. When Drew's funeral was over, that flag had been carefully folded, stripes into stars, until it formed a perfect triangle. Then it was given to me.

I liked to think that the honor, the sorrow, and compassion of all the law-enforcement officers present that day had been folded into the flag, tucked safely into the tidy creases that the state troopers made with their sweet hands before handing it to the governor to present to Drew's widow "on behalf of the people of Maine."

The flag was now kept carefully at home, and of course, it had not been unfolded since that day.

"Dad's flag is the best thing we have to give," Zach said. The other three children agreed.

So the following day, a crazy lady appeared at the Thomaston post office. She had a package, nicely wrapped and neatly addressed, and she paid the postage, but the postmaster had to pry it out of her hands before he could send it.

It was hard to let it go. We thought we would never see it again—but Zach was right: It was the best thing, the most loving prayer, we had. So we sent it to New York.

About two years after 9/11, a package arrived in my mailbox. The return address read NEW YORK CITY POLICE DEPARTMENT. Detectives from the NYPD had taken Drew's flag down from where it had been flying above the evidence pile at Staten Island. They had folded it into a tidy triangle, wrapped it up, and sent it home.

Again I thought of the sorrow, the honor, the compassion folded into the flag before it was mailed back to me.

I was reminded of Drew's flag when I attended a funeral for Portland Police Sergeant Robert Johnsey. There, before the broad blue sea of Portland police uniforms, two officers folded Rob Johnsey's flag. I watched their hands: How tender they were, how gently they held the triangle of cloth against their hearts before presenting it, on behalf of the people of Maine, to Carol Johnsey to hold against her own heart. All that honor, all that love, folded into a triangle of stars.

The package containing Drew's folded flag came home from New York about five years ago now. And the flag had not been unfolded since, until the day I went to the Maine law-enforcement memorial service as a chaplain—and a survivor. On that day, Drew's flag unfurled and flew over all the assembled officers standing at parade rest; it flew on behalf of Maine's law-enforcement family and on behalf of the citizens of Maine. It flew for those who mourned the fallen, and for every man and woman who wore a badge above an undefended heart.

It was by far the best prayer I have ever offered or ever will. And it was a flag.

A Tibetan Buddhist will write her prayers on pieces of cotton and hang the cloth where the wind can find it. The prayer flags wave, and the prayers themselves are carried by the wind all over the earth.

Buddhist prayers are also written on a prayer wheel, and every time the wheel completes a rotation, the prayer is "spoken" and sent forth.

I told my children this, and Ellie immediately wanted to know whether she could tie a prayer to the spokes of her bicycle, so that prayers for loving kindness might go into the world every time she took a ride around the neighborhood. Charmed, I immediately imagined all the rotating circles I could add a prayer to. I rejected hubcaps, the salad spinner, and a Frisbee.

As it is a tool for the creation of beauty, Simon's pottery wheel seemed much better suited to be a bearer and speaker of the sacred. *And when I finally get around to learning to spin wool into yarn,* I thought happily, *I will ask Simon to carve a prayer into my hand-carved wooden spinning wheel . . .* and whoops! This suddenly sounded suspiciously like the bias that had me pawing through all the blank books at my local bookstore back in the day, searching for the one that looked most "spiritual" (e.g., gold-encrusted, faux-ancient, and, not coincidentally, expensive). Forget the image of the hand-carved spinning wheel, or at least set it to one side. If you take serious joy in Frisbee, cooking, or cars, it is that joy that will lift the prayer.

Speaking of circles: "Suppose we were to take a compass and insert the point and draw the outline of a circle," a sixth-century Christian monk named Dorotheos of Gaza suggested. "The center point is the same distance from any point on the circumference . . . Let us suppose that this circle is the world, and that God himself is the center. The straight lines drawn from the circumference to the center are the lives of human beings. . . . Let us assume for the sake of the analogy that to move toward God, then, human beings move from the circumference along the various radii of the circle to the center. But at the same time, the closer they are to God, the closer they become to one another; and the closer they are to one another, the closer they become to God."

And, of course, "the opposite is also true," writes scholar Roberta C. Bondi, who quotes Dorotheos in a fine little book about the early Church fathers, *To Love as God Loves*. "As we move toward God, we move toward other people, and as we move away from people, we also move away from God."

This image is fun to draw, and perhaps the drawing itself could serve as a kind of prayer, "an approach to God" in itself.

Or—what the heck—the kids can make a board game out of it on a rainy day ("Made cookies for a sick neighbor! Two spaces closer to God!," "Oops, kicked sister in the shin, take three steps back," "Blasphemed loudly when kicked in the shins," etc.) and play it (pray it?) with their friends.

Maine's coast is, famously, a rocky one. Our beaches are covered with stones, which suits me fine, as I prefer walking around looking for interesting rocks to lying around on the sand. (This sounds like a moral distinction, but it's because I burn easily. I have no problem lying around in my house.) When I was growing up, we looked for "lucky stones," ones with a stripe of contrasting mineral wrapped completely around. More recently, I've gone out of my way to look for stones striped in two directions, forming a cross on one or more planes—I was surprised at how often such geological wonders occur. I save pocket-size cross stones to give to Christian friends who are enduring a time of worry or grief.

"When things get better," I tell them, "you can give it away to someone who needs it more." Holding the stone is good. Knowing you will someday pass it on to someone else is good, too.

My friend Monica found a big cross stone, about the size of a brick, on the beach and brought it home to give me. It adorns

Simon's flower garden most of the time, but I have taken it with me to Easter services at my church to be used in a very simple ritual.

The stone begins at the front of the sanctuary, where I explain that it will be passed hand to hand and pew to pew until it has made its way throughout the whole church and back to the altar. "When you receive the stone, I invite you to say the name of someone dear to you who has died. You can say the name out loud or silently. When you have said the name, you may pass the stone to your neighbor."

That's it: the whole ritual. The stone gets passed, hand to hand, and the names are said. People cry a little. They pat the stone before they hand it along. Some people don't say anything out loud, simply pausing for a moment before letting the weight move on.

I was particularly moved during a service in which a mentally handicapped man held the stone up to his mouth, as if it were a telephone, and shouted his mother's name loudly, as if whoever was on the other end of the stone-line were hard of hearing.

By now the cross stone in my garden has had hundreds of, perhaps a thousand or more, names spoken lovingly over it. It sits among the ferns, obdurate, unchanged, the cross the remnant of long-ago quartz intrusions into a granite substrate. The stone's relationship to grief and love remains merely and profoundly mineral: It is a rock. And it is a prayer.

"Beware of practicing your piety before others in order to be seen by them," Jesus advised. Just as real charity doesn't require an announcement or a brass plaque, true prayer doesn't demand a witness. "Go into your room and shut the door" (Matthew 6: 1–6).

My husband, Simon, doesn't generally go into his room and close the door to pray. For one thing, it's now *our* room, and for another, we share the house with a bunch of teenagers who are shockingly disinclined to regard a closed door as an obstacle to instant familial intimacy (unless it's their own door).

When my husband and I were first dating, the day he included me in his prayers was a sweet benchmark. He didn't tell me what sort of prayers these were, or even who else was on his list, only that I was among them, and that this was significant for him, a cause for joy.

Simon prays as he runs. Strenuous exercise pretty much guarantees solitude, at least for a man married to me. For another thing, it offers genuine privacy. Although our neighbors and passersby can see him run by, what they see is a man staying in shape, not a man saying his prayers.

Running, Simon adds, is also something he does entirely for his own sake. He loves to cook, but his family and friends will receive the food. He loves to create beautiful things, but others will view and take pleasure in them. So Simon prays as he runs.

His formula, he tells me, is simple, as befits a prayer that must compete with aching calf muscles for the mind's attention: *May I be peaceful, happy, and light in body and spirit. May I be safe and free from injury.* He can insert as many names as he likes: *May my daughter be ... May my friend be ... May the president be ...* And now: *May Kate be, too!*

It is not a Catholic prayer, although Simon was raised Catholic. His mother gave him a book by Thich Nhat Hanh that had this prayer in it. Thea is Catholic, but she uses this prayer, too, along with the Ave Maria and the Pater Noster.

"But really, I believe, as the Desert Fathers and the Mystics would say, that there is only one prayer," Thea says. "It is to say 'yes' and 'thank you.'" There are many words and wordless ways to say it, as my friend and poet Alla Renée Bozarth reminds us:

WHAT IS PRAYER?

... Be awake to the Life that is loving you
and sing your prayer, laugh your prayer,
dance your prayer, run
and weep and sweat your prayer,
sleep your prayer, eat your prayer,

175

paint, sculpt, hammer and read your prayer,
sweep, dig, rake, drive and hoe your prayer,
garden and farm and build and clean your prayer,
wash, iron, vacuum, sew, embroider and pickle your prayer,
compute, touch, bend and fold but never delete
or mutilate your prayer.

Learn and play your prayer,
work and rest your prayer,
fast and feast your prayer,
argue, talk, whisper, listen and shout your prayer,
groan and moan and spit and sneeze your prayer,
swim and hunt and cook your prayer,
digest and become your prayer.

Release and recover your prayer.
Breathe your prayer.
Be your prayer.*

---

* From "What is Prayer?" in *Moving to the Edge of the World,* by Alla Renée
Bozarth, iUniverse 2000. All rights reserved.

19

Praying with Your Body

Serene, exquisitely groomed, draped in a monk's robe or a nun's habit—fashion seems key, here—I am kneeling before some divinely beautiful thing (an altar, an icon, a window admitting only a perfect clarity of light) with my hands perhaps upraised in welcome or folded before my breasts (pert) in graceful supplication.

When, according to this vision, I am finished with my prayers, I continue my consciousness-building devotions by taking a spiritual bath (remembering all the ways that water is used in traditional religious practice: baptism, holy water, the sacred Ganges). Without a trace of irony, I use expensive soaps with names like Shanti or Moon Goddess that smell fabulous and yet somehow underline the idea that I am not in the tub merely to wash my armpits or shave my legs. This is *spirituality,* not grooming.

After I've bathed, and still with a serene expression, my brow uncreased as any Botox-infused matron's, I'll go have some tantric sex with my husband. This is, after all, a fantasy.

Realistically, said husband might spoil the mood by wishing aloud that I had shaved my legs, and with that thought, I am again myself, a middle-aged white woman burdened with time limits, cellulite, a human spouse, and a bathtub that will need to be scrubbed before any sort of bathing, spiritual or otherwise, can take place in it. If I wait for the ideal time and environment, let alone the ideal self, I'll die before a single prayer gets said.

God bless my husband, my bathtub, my bed . . .
My home and my body, my heart and my head . . .

Congregationalism—the root of my own religious tradition—generally discourages wild, lush, sensual religious experiences. The Congregationalists have been known, rather, for impeccable decorum and politesse.

Calvinist Protestants in eighteenth-century America built churches with tall windows of clear glass, the better to receive the stern clarity of God's light. They sorted themselves into box pews, where the seats met the seat backs at an uncompromising and anatomically inhuman ninety-degree angle. This added an extra element of Spartan rigor to those who listened, perforce, to sermons of three and four hours' duration.

Both Martin Luther and John Calvin asserted the primacy of the Word over all other manifestations of God's presence and works in the world. Hence the dramatically elevated Protestant pulpit, buttressed to take the weight of an overlarge King James Version.

According to these, my spiritual ancestors, the appropriate response to hearing the Word is to maintain a posture of dignified attentiveness. If something itches, thou shalt not scratch. We will read our prayers and do a little restrained singing (with those who sing off-key encouraged to lip-synch), but we aren't going to laugh, dance, run, or prostrate ourselves in church, and we are most certainly not going to perspire. If a congregant happens to take ill, give birth, or die, everyone shall pretend not to notice.

Should Jesus appear and bring the dead congregant back to life in some noticeable and, one hopes, not too untidy miracle, we will respond graciously. Thank you so much, Mr. Christ, might we offer you some more comfortable church attire? A necktie, perhaps? Do, please, join us for coffee hour.

My denomination, Unitarian Universalism, is a direct descendant of New England Congregationalism, so I approve of the elevation of the Word and enjoy preaching my guest sermons from an elevated pulpit, even if I did preach once from a pulpit so high it gave me a nosebleed.

Maybe it comes from all that upward gazing, but mine remains a stiff-necked people. Even though we have broken away from our Calvinist roots and now draw eagerly upon the wisdom of all the world's traditions, we do not bow our heads, we do not kneel, and we do not surrender. In New England, Unitarian Universalist congregations often occupy the old places of worship, so whether we have chosen to be frozen or not, we remain confined in our box pews. Forget prostrations: Even standing up to sing a hymn means risking a banged knee.

If the Congregational aesthetic is what you're used to, visiting a place where worship demands actual movement can make you feel like a total spaz. This is especially true in those exuberantly Christian churches where people wave their arms in the air and dance in the aisles, but even attending the funeral of a game warden's Catholic dad made me feel clumsily Protestant. I fumbled with the little kneeling step for what seemed like hours until I figured out how to make it clank down into position, and upon kneeling, I became hideously self-conscious about the soles of my shoes, now so strangely exposed to public view.

During prayer, one is supposed to keep one's eyes closed, so I couldn't even cast a protective eye around myself or try to catch the noseyparker who was sneaking a censorious peek at my soles.

Maybe I should just stick to those denominations that allow me to be a pew potato. It's what I'm used to. And because I don't really have a good relationship with my body—I tend to forget I own one—I'm a klutz, and prayer only makes it worse.

Doubtless, it is a matter of genetics. In my family of origin, none of us has a body, at least not body as body. My mother could never understand why anyone played sports or went skiing ("up and down the same mountain all day long!"). It was considered self-indulgent to diet, to fuss about one's hair, or use more than the bare minimum of grooming products in your twice-weekly bath. We assured one another that this was not laziness but the sign of a refined intellect. (Who needs the *corpore sano* if you've got the *mens sana*?) The human body exists to keep the human brain from dragging on the ground.

So among the many astonishing revelations of my life has been the way the body—my body, the bodies of accident victims and their families, the bodies of game wardens—assumes center stage in those rare moments when I experience grace.

A Catholic would doubtless be amused at my astonishment: Of course the body is central. Why do you think the Church is called the Corpus Christi, a place we keep the Body of Christ hanging on our crosses or waiting as the Host? Why do you think we were given the Body to take into our own bodies; why would God incarnate ("become meat") at all if ignoring the body were either desirable or possible for spiritual practice? If God experienced human life through human flesh and expressed divine love through feeding, healing, and restoring human bodies, what makes you think you can skip that part? Jesus lived and loved in and through his body; could there be another, better Way than His? (Imaginary Catholics always crush me in our imaginary arguments.)

Because Maine's game wardens are forced to confront suffering and death in the course of their work, and because these confrontations take their toll on human psychological—that is, neurological—well-being, the Maine Warden Service boasts not only a chaplain but also a critical incident stress management team. Following an event that is more than usually stressful, gruesome, or sad by law-enforcement standards (civilian standards would have us doing a debriefing every week), the affected wardens will gather together, and specially trained peers will lead them through what is really a more structured version of the sorts of conversations human beings have been engaging in since human life (and thus human suffering) began. If I had my druthers, I'd have all of these debriefings take place around a campfire, to emphasize the antiquity of such rituals, as well as to allow men accustomed to living outdoors to feel more at home.

As it is, these meetings generally take place in a conference room in one or another Warden Service district headquarters and, if we're lucky, offer some sense of privacy, comfort, and intimacy. There is always food to eat and plenty of water to emphasize the benefits of "remaining hydrated."

At the conclusion of the session, the team leader gives the participating wardens a little lecture about the effects of stress on the body, together with suggestions for how stressed bodies can be cared for so as to hasten a return to normal functioning.

It's something I have to learn and relearn myself: We are accustomed to thinking of our minds as independent of our bodies, yet everything our bodies do, including thinking and feeling, is mediated by brain chemistry, and what is experienced by the body provokes changes in that chemistry.

"When some aspect of an incident is really 'sticking' with a warden," I tell the members of the CISM team, "it will express itself through his body. Watch what he does with his body while he's telling his story."

A game warden might say, "The guy was right there! I almost stepped on him!" His wide eyes will fix themselves on a point in an imaginary forest floor while his foot comes up and hesitates in the air.

"I took the kid out from under the ice," another warden will announce quite matter-of-factly—but every time he says it, his arms will make a lifting movement, then form themselves into a cradle.

Powerful emotional, spiritual, and even intellectual experience insist on expressing themselves through our bodies. Some cultures allow for more action, but even the extremely restrained will be unable to prevent their hands from trembling, their faces from turning pale. So if our prayers have power—that is, if they are or should be more than words, more meaningful than a nursery rhyme or a grocery list—then our bodies must be part of the prayer. It is hard to even imagine prayer without imagining that the body of the person praying has assumed a certain specific pose. The pose can serve not only as an announcement of the act of prayer, it might also evoke—even replace—the prayer itself. Religious paintings are full of images of human beings and holy beings praying, but the painter doesn't give us words. He or she doesn't need to; the positions of the bodies speak for themselves.

So it is worth paying attention to what your body does when you pray, either alone or with others. (When my family says grace, for instance, we hold hands, bow our heads, and close our eyes.) Chances are very good that your body does *something*.

"Join me, as you will, in the spirit of prayer," I say before offering words at a Warden Service awards supper or some other ceremonial occasion, and at once, all the bodies in the room change. The knees align, the spines straighten, hands are put to rest on knees or in laps. Whether they intend to pray or simply to wait politely for the prayer to end, their bodies assume an attentiveness that to me is lovely and even entirely sufficient. My redundant words emerge humbly into air already filled with prayer.

It's me, I guess, talking to myself, but I like to think of the voice in my head as the Still, Small Voice of biblical renown. Certainly, like the voice that challenged Moses, it never tells me what I want to hear.

I hate to break this to you, Kate, says SSV, *but it is a little late to resist. You're ordained. You have given your whole life to me. So tell me again why it is you don't kneel?*

I could think of no answer that didn't sound stuck up. So now I am learning to kneel when I pray. I can't say I like it—I'm middle-aged, and my knees make alarming noises when asked to bear my weight—but I'm doing it. What the hell.

Kneeling in prayer is a modified form of ritual prostration and, as such, has analogues in the *sajdah* prostrations of Muslims at prayer, the *panipata* prostration of Buddhism, the *Mutha Dheek* of Sikhs, and the *zemnoy poklon* of the Eastern Orthodox. It is akin to yoga's child pose and to the way a minion would kowtow (literally, "knock head") before the emperor in China. For that matter, should I ever decide to play out one of my vague but recurrent spiritual fantasies and become a nun, holy orders would be conferred upon me during a service requiring a full and prayerful prostration.

These ritual poses are virtually identical in anatomical positioning (toes, knees, hands, and forehead in contact with the ground, eyes closed) and in their symbolic meaning. Uniformly, they are understood as signaling extreme respect and complete submission.

The symbolism is uniform because it is anything but arbitrary. Prone is the pose into which a police officer will place a dangerous suspect precisely because it is maximally disabling. His open hands are demonstrably weaponless; his lowered head and closed eyes deprive him of his most effective defensive senses. Unable to effectively track the movements of others, he will likewise be incapable of anticipating and deflecting blows that might be aimed at his defenseless neck.

Like a puppy who rolls over and exposes her unprotected tummy to the teeth of a larger dog, or like the chimpanzee (a cousin of ours, remember) who submits to the alpha male—for all the world like a Buddhist pilgrim doing a little *wui tou di* on the way to Lhasa—the adherent who bows, genuflects, or lays down his body in prayer is offering unconditional surrender to God.

On the other hand, if you lose consciousness, your body will get into a prone position as quickly as possible, which is to say that you will fall flat on your face. In that position, gravity no longer resists the flow of blood to the brain, and the chances of recovery improve. Get it? Lose consciousness, flop down into *sajdah*, and— Allah willing—consciousness returns!

When we human beings are told that someone we love is dead, we assume the position, or try to. Our knees buckle, we surrender, and we go down. If you are among those who deeply love what is mortal, you might as well get used to going down: You will not stand for this. Perhaps prostrations are a part of worship in so many religions so that we may practice, performing deliberately in prayer what we shall do when the all-consuming, consciousness-engulfing blow is struck, and for the same reason. We descend because that is the way to rising again.

"Are you all right? Do you feel sick to your stomach?" I asked the young man sitting behind me in the warden's truck. The young man's father had drowned in a river in western Maine the night before. The dive team had just recovered the body, and the warden at the wheel was following the hearse over a hilly country road. The young man was quite composed. He, rather than his mother, had been the one to identify the body and sit with it on the river-bank while we waited for the call from the medical examiner that would give us permission to let the funeral director remove it. Now he was squashed into the backseat of a pickup in a space excavated from the warden's equipment. He gave no sign of discomfort, so I am not sure why I turned, put my hand briefly on his knee, and asked if he was getting carsick.

"No," he said, smiling bravely. "I'm okay."

A few weeks later, I received a letter from this young man, asking me to convey his thanks to the warden divers who had located and recovered his father's body. He thanked me as well, for the "comfort and support" I had offered him, but specifically, for asking him that question. "I was actually feeling sort of sick," the young man confessed. "Though I didn't want to say so, but it meant a lot to me that you were concerned enough about me to ask."

You never know what people will remember from a day of sudden tragedy. Or rather, you do know: They will remember that you took care of them. They will remember that you took care of their physical well-being. "I remember your hand on my shoulder . . ." "I was so touched when you brought me that bottle of water . . ." "I could tell you were right behind me, ready to support me if I started to fall apart . . ."

"Love one another," the man said. How else can I love you but by loving your body with my body? The human body is the human being.

Here is a proposition everyone agrees on: Jesus of Nazareth was a human being.

For Christians, Jesus was and is divine as well, but the orthodox will insist that Jesus was not a god wearing a mask. He was a real man, fully divine, fully human. To claim otherwise is to be guilty of a heresy (specifically Docetism).

So Jesus was as human as you are, as human as I am, fully and completely human.

There is no reason to restrict our definition of "human being" to a first, fourth, or even nineteenth-century understanding of human biology. The Christian understanding of Jesus as fully human cannot be an anachronism. Fifteen hundred years or so before Harvey explained the human heart as a functioning pump, Jesus had a four-chambered heart that pumped warm blood. He had an immune system with the usual complement of leukocytes and lymphocytes. He had myelinated nerves and a spinal cord and there, within the hard bone box of his skull, he had about a pound and a half of putty-colored aspic: Jesus had a human brain.

It was a good brain. People noticed that right from the start. Young Jesus' synapses fired so swiftly in the synagogue one day that the wise elders were impressed. "Smart cookie!" they said, or words to that effect.

Others would occasionally have their doubts.

Take the Pharisee in Luke, Chapter 7. He's thrown a dinner party for Jesus, and a prostitute comes into the house to join the guests. That's bad enough, but when she catches sight of Jesus, she begins to misbehave. She stands behind him weeping, and she lets her hair down—right there in front of everyone!—and she begins to bathe his feet with her tears and to dry them with her hair. And she keeps kissing his feet and anointing them with ointment.

When the Pharisee saw this, he became quite uncomfortable. He said to himself, "If this man were a prophet, he would have known who and what kind of woman this is who is touching him . . ."

Luke 7:37–39

A prophet, after all, doesn't know just the future. A prophet knows the truth. In truth, there was Jesus the Divine, supine on a couch, while a professional sex toy slobbered all over his feet. How smart can this guy be, the Pharisee wonders, if Jesus doesn't know what this looks like?

No mention is made in the New Testament of Jesus' brain, which is not too surprising, since even the best ancient physicians considered the brain an uninteresting organ. Still, there are a lot of references to Jesus' feet. Disciples, penitents, supplicants, and bystanders throw themselves at his feet. His friend Mary sits enraptured at his feet to imbibe the better part, and later, in place of that prostitute, she will wash, anoint, and kiss his feet.

This gets interesting when you consider that in the Bible the word "foot" not only refers to the anatomical appendage but also carries a variety of symbolic meanings. There's the image of conquest and dominion: In Psalm 8:6 the phrase "put all things under his feet" corresponds to an actual practice of conquerors in ancient times. Paul tells the Corinthians that Jesus will have the cosmos "under his feet" any one of these days. Picture the winner in a professional wrestling match or, for that matter, the big-game hunter—they pose with one foot on the fallen, don't they? It's easy to see how practical reality and symbol became intertwined. When Mary sits at Jesus' feet, she is both yielding to a practical reality—no chairs—and submitting herself to his, that is, God's dominion.

Similarly, the act of washing Jesus' feet is part of practical, Ancient Near East hospitality—the roads were dusty—and also has to do with humility before God. (This hospitable foot-washing, by the by, was generally done by women or slaves.)

Underneath it all, feet are transportation. *How beautiful are the feet of those who bring the good news!* Paul writes to the Romans (Romans 10:15).

There is a Christian publishing house, Beautiful Feet Books, that takes its name from this line. They put out *D'Auliere's Book of Greek Myths*, along with well-illustrated biographies of Ben Franklin and Abraham Lincoln for children. I went online to try to locate a title one day. I typed the name of the publisher into the search engine, "Beautiful Feet," and was promptly rewarded with thousands of websites devoted to foot fetishes.

Wouldn't you just know it? Some sickos out there in cyberspace have ruined a perfectly wholesome Bible verse by attaching it to their creepy little websites! It's not as if there's anything kinky about Christian feet, not as if there's anything sexual about that, um, prostitute . . . washing and massaging and . . . y'know . . . kissing Jesus' feet . . .

With reluctant candor, the *Abingdon Bible Dictionary* states that among the biblical metaphors involving feet, we must include "the euphemistic use of the term 'feet' for [the genitals]." See, for example, Isaiah 6:2, Judges 3:24, etc.

Jesus had feet. He also had "feet." But the important thing here is that Jesus had a human brain. I've got the same sort of brain jiggling around inside my head: If you were to saw off the top of my skull, my brain would look just like Jesus'. Brains haven't changed in over two thousand years, after all. Whack the back end of my brain with a club, and I'm blind. Alter the chemistry by a few molecules here and there, and I'm nuts or "possessed by demons." Injure the frontal lobe and I won't be me anymore (though it won't worry me much).

If this is true for you and for me, it is also true for Jesus and for each of the disciples, all of them possessors of human brains.

Human brains are used to process information. Nerves transmit chemical messages from the various regions of the body to receptor sites within the brain, and those sites translate the chemical messages into our human reality. Some body areas and organs have a lot of receptor sites in the brain—we call these "sensitive" areas: the fingertips, the lips. Other body parts—the shoulder, for instance—have relatively few receptor sites and are, from our point of view, comparatively insensitive.

The brain's receptor sites are organized in ways that may seem arbitrary to us. The receptor site for, say, the ear isn't next to the site for the jaw, even though jaws and ears are neighbors on the outside. Instead, the auditory nerve receptor lies quite close to something called the oculomotor nerve nucleus. This is something you don't particularly need to know unless your auditory nerve is damaged, which frequently forces axons in the auditory nerve receptor site to invade the site for the oculomotor nerve. Hearing and seeing then get mixed up—when you use your eyes, you hear sounds. It's a disorienting experience.

Even without damage, the neighborliness of receptor sites in the brain has its effects. The proximity of some sites would appear to encourage behaviors that enhance survival. Take nipples, for instance. The receptor site for the female nipple is located smack dab next to the site for the genitals. Breastfeeding an infant thus becomes a mildly—or, in some cases, extremely—pleasurable experience for the mother. This makes women more inclined to breastfeed frequently, which makes for fat, happy babies.

If you are one of the many people who find music a profound, essential component of worship, it may interest you to know that the receptor site used in processing music is right next door to that area in the brain identified with religious experience—what neurologists sometimes call "the God Module."

And speaking of God: The receptor site in the male brain that receives nerve impulses from the genitals is snuggled right in next to the receptor site *for the feet*. Knowing this, take a look at Chapter 13 in the Gospel of John.

> And during supper Jesus . . . got up from the table. He laid aside his garments and girded himself with a small towel. Then he poured water into a basin and began to wash the disciples' feet and to wipe them with the towel that was tied around him. He

came to Simon Peter, who said to him "Lord, are you going to wash my feet?" Jesus answered: "You do not know now what I am doing, but later you will understand." Peter said, "You will never wash my feet." Jesus said, "Unless I wash you, you have no share with me." Jesus washed his feet, and Simon Peter said to him, "Lord, not my feet only, but also my hands and my head." After Jesus had washed their feet, had put on his clothes and had returned to the table, Jesus said to them, "Do you know what I have done to you?"

Do you know what I have done to you?
He doesn't do it to some and not to others. Jesus washes the feet of each of the disciples. Even Judas gets his feet washed.

So when he comes to Simon Peter, it's not as if Simon Peter doesn't know what's up. He has watched as the others, in turn, have had it done to them. This isn't a real question, "Lord, are you going to wash my feet?" It's an expression of intense anxiety.

Perhaps even watching the act has been too much. Simon is resisting an exquisite intimacy; Lord, you will never wash my feet. But Simon Peter always has a hard time with full commitment, doesn't he? He always has to be dragged into the Full Monty.

Jesus answers him: You don't get it now, but someday you will. Unless I wash you, you have no share with me.

So he washes him, and Simon Peter, now lost in love, says to him, "Lord, not my feet only, but also my hands and my head." Wash me all over, Jesus.

Do you know what I have done to you?
Are you, at this moment, uncomfortable? Are you asking yourself why I am putting a sexual spin on this delicate moment wherein Jesus was giving his final instructions, the last living signs of his deep humility, his example of pure and selfless love?

Simon Peter was a human being. Jesus was a human being. The author of the Gospel of John was a human being. All of these human beings, these men, had feet and they had brains. Not once but many times in the New Testament, someone—a prostitute?—is anointing, massaging, weeping over, kissing Jesus' feet. No wonder the Pharisee was unnerved. No wonder Simon Peter is taken aback when his Lord and his God starts stripping off his clothes. "You will never wash my feet!" he cries. It is too intimate an act for him to accept.

Receive, says Jesus. Just receive me.

Let's be clear: I am not claiming that Jesus was on the make. I'm not declaring that Jesus was gay, or bi, or anything but this: Jesus was a human being and—if we take his divinity as seriously as we take his humanity—Jesus was love, incarnating before his disciples' very eyes.

After three years of schlepping around with Jesus, Simon Peter thought he knew what the relationship with God was all about. But now Jesus was taking him way out of his comfort zone. If Simon Peter were a brain surgeon—okay, this is a stretch, but anyway—you would almost hear him asking: Can't my relationship with this incredible person confine itself to my cerebral cortex, the part of my brain that likes to think it's in control? Is Jesus not even going to stop at my mammalian brain, where my emotions lie . . . Oh, Lord, must your divine love truly penetrate all the way down, down to my ancient and reptilian core, that place wherein are found not just breath and heartbeat but the sweaty, slimy secrets I would as soon keep hidden?

You tell me, says Jesus. What part of you is off-limits to God?

Sunday after Sunday, in the Communion inaugurated in the first three Gospels, Christians receive the blood and body of Christ in their very mouths. Presumably, the bread is intended to signify the whole body of Christ, not only the parts we feel more comfortable discussing, and this in turn is a feast that nourishes our whole selves. What part of an incarnate God would you not take into yourself?

Washing, massaging, and anointing a man's feet carries a lot of meanings about welcome and service, about crossing lines of gender and class, about humility and love. And by the evidence of both human neurology and sacred scripture, washing a man's feet is an erotic act.

You can do whatever you want to do, theologically speaking, with this information. If it confuses or upsets you, pretend not to know. That's a time-honored strategy in religious life, so you'll have lots of company. There are plenty of Christian churches that have opted to wash one another's hands on Maundy Thursday ("It's less messy," a Congregational minister assured me with perhaps unconscious accuracy). There are others that don't wash anything at all.

WWJD? Jesus offered an intimate act of love that involved the whole human body—his body, your body—from head to toe, brain to feet, and in so doing pressed the anxious Peter, and therefore all of us, to question the limits we place on loving and being loved. You are fully human so as one human being to another, let me leave you with this question: What part of you lies beyond or beneath the pleasure, comfort, and inescapable demands of love? Is it your sexuality? Your scars? Your wallet? Your politics? Your past?

Simon Peter begins with resistance and ends in ecstasy: not just my feet, Lord, but also my hands and my head. Wash me all over, Jesus . . . wash me all over.

PART FIVE

The Word

20

Prayers in Mixed Company

A colleague who is a theologically conservative Christian minister serves as a National Guard chaplain here in Maine. I asked him about the language he uses for his public prayers, given that he is so often asked to pray before groups of people from many different religious backgrounds.

"I use the word 'God,'" he said. "But I don't use 'Jesus.'"

"Really?" I said. "You don't conclude with 'we pray this in the name of our Lord, Jesus Christ'?"

"Nope," he answered. "I can do that at my own church, because I know that everyone in the pews would affirm it. But if I were to claim that a mixed group of soldiers are all praying in the name of Jesus when I know full well that at least some of those guys aren't praying in the name of Jesus, or praying at all, then I'm not really praying anymore, either. I'm lying. Worse yet, I'm lying to God."

"Eek."

"Besides," he went on, "I don't need to tell God whose name I'm praying in. God already knows."

"But you will use the word 'God,'" I said carefully, making sure.

"The word 'God' is pretty elastic. It allows for a lot of different interpretations, and even if some of the ways some soldiers might be interpreting that word would seem wrong to me, or unscriptural, so be it. It isn't my job at that moment to make sure everyone is praying correctly. It's my job to stand there and pray with them as best I can."

I found this a refreshing and very useful conversation. He had helped me to sort out my own approach to praying in front of large and diverse groups, something I am called upon to do with surprising frequency as a minister and a law-enforcement chaplain.

But what about when I am praying alone? To whom do I pray? To God.

I have no doubt that my National Guard chaplain friend would consider my understanding of God incomplete and unscriptural. I'd probably have a bone or two to pick with his understanding of God, too, if it came to that. Still, I think he would be willing to pray with me, just as I would be to pray with him.

In a poem entitled "On Prayer," Czeslaw Milosz answers an imaginary atheist with love, "You ask me how to pray to someone who is not," he writes. "All I know is that prayer constructs a velvet bridge." To set foot on that bridge requires not certainty but deep humility. If the other end of the bridge turns out to rest on nothing, well then, walking the bridge together in love shall be a fine and sufficient gift.

The first time I was asked to offer a prayer to a large group of people of varying religious backgrounds was some months after September 11. I was invited to participate in an interfaith service held in a small town. Various prayers would be said for various actors: as a law-enforcement chaplain, I was to offer the prayer for the rescuers (firefighters and police officers).

The service was held in the gymnasium of the town's high school, which is both an ordinary public high school for the town and a quasi-private academy attended by students from all over the world. Most townspeople were expected to attend, along with a substantial contingent of foreign teenagers, at least some of whom were from Muslim countries.

My children came to the service with me. Because I wanted to keep an eye on them, I had them sit in the front row, right in front of the lectern that would serve as our pulpit.

What they remember most vividly about that evening was the prayer offered by the pastor of an institution called something like the Church of the Solid Rock of Jesus. The pastor of this group had taken on the most difficult part of the service: He had to lead the prayer for our enemies. After expressing a brief hope that perhaps our enemies—Osama bin Laden and the leaders of the Taliban— might become Christians (perhaps even along the lines laid out by the Church of the Solid Rock of Jesus?), the pastor began to cry out for vengeance.

"Turn their hearts, oh Lord," he said, "but if their hearts will not be turned, then SMITE THEM! SMITE THEM! CRUSH THEM!"

I was seated behind the pastor and so was spared at least some of the force of this peroration, but my children's faces expressed such alarm that I had to bite the insides of my cheeks to suppress a burst of unseemly laughter.

"SEEK THEM OUT, LORD, SEEK THEM IN THEIR HIDING PLACES AND CRUSH THEM BENEATH YOUR HEEL AS YOU MIGHT A SERPENT'S HEAD, SMITE THEM AND CAST THEM DOWN INTO THE FIERY PIT WITH ALL OTHER FOUL UNBE- LIEF AND UNGODLINESS," he raved, his flushed jowls shudder- ing with fury, his spittle showering the front row of seats.

It was memorable. Still, I had some sympathy for the pastor of the Church of the Solid Rock of Jesus: The Catholic priest was going to say his prayer for the victims, the Baptist would pray for their families, and the Methodist would offer his prayer for our men and women in uniform, so praying for the enemies was unquestion- ably the toughest assignment. Mine was the easiest, given my pas- sionate affection for emergency service providers, especially police officers.

When the invitation to participate in the prayer service was extended, I noted that this putatively interfaith service was really going to be merely *interdenominational*. With a Unitarian Universalist providing only a pale hint of diversity, the clergy would be wall-to-wall Christians up on the dais speaking to a crowd that was certain to be a much more complex mixture. So I prefaced my prayer this way:

"Before I offer a prayer for the rescuers, I would like to extend my gratitude for the tolerance and patience of those of you whose religious tradition may not be adequately represented by the clergy assembled here, or who may not be religious at all.

"I am convinced that you have all already offered the finest prayer there could be: You are here. We are together. It is a great honor to stand before you and say with mere words what you have already expressed with greater eloquence simply by your presence. Thank you.

"Join me, if you will, in a spirit of prayer or meditation . . ."

This didn't strike me as a particularly daring or controversial sentiment. If none of the other ministers had thought to articulate it, I was sure that was an oversight. After the prayer service, I introduced my kids to all the clergy (Zach complimented the pastor of the Solid Rock of Jesus on having delivered the most exciting prayer), and we ate more than our share of the refreshments on offer, then went home.

The following morning, I received a call from a member of the audience: Apparently, I had caused a small kerfuffle. Many townspeople who had been at the prayer service, including many students, were expressing what seemed to me a disproportionate gratitude for even so fleeting a reference to the diversity that had been represented there. Meanwhile, some churchgoers were asking their own ministers why only "that woman" had thought to say something about it.

At the risk of causing more such controversy, I preface my remarks with a similar acknowledgment whenever I am asked to lead a prayer or give a sermon before a large, obviously diverse group; for example, when I was asked to give the invocation at the National Law Enforcement Officers Memorial's twentieth annual candlelight vigil in Washington, D.C.

Judiciary Square was packed with police officers, survivors of fallen officers, politicians, and assorted dignitaries numbering over twenty thousand. Imagine the range of religious backgrounds and orientations. To name the obvious seemed then, and seems now, simple, truthful, and loving, and therefore . . . prayer.

21

Praying with Enemies

Ram Dass gives a great little homily about an altar he had erected in his home to hold pictures of some of his favorite avatars: Krishna, Jesus, Gandhi, and Martin Luther King, Jr.

Each morning Ram Dass would arise and, before moving on with his day, pause before the altar, bow, and greet each avatar in turn: "Good morning, Krishna! Good morning, Jesus! Good morning, Mr. Gandhi! Good morning, Reverend Dr. King!"

As a form of moral discipline, Ram Dass also kept images on the altar of people he didn't like so much. Then–Secretary of Defense Caspar Weinberger, for example.

He might have had to grit his teeth to do it, but Ram Dass forced himself to bow and say, "Good morning, Secretary Weinberger."

On hearing this story, I thought about whose pictures I might put on an altar to greet as I started the day.

Then I realized: I have something like this already. Above the desk in my office, I have a little icon of Father Mychal; a picture of Jesus (arms missing); a portrait of Sophie Scholl (cofounder and martyr of the White Rose, a student resistance group in Nazi Germany); a photograph of a Danish fishing boat that was used to smuggle Jews to safety during the German occupation of Denmark; and a portrait of my husband, Simon's, hands, covered with clay, forming the delicate lip of a porcelain bowl.

There are no images of anyone I dislike. No politicians I disagree with, no ex-boyfriends, no serial killers or brutal dictators.

Nor was I inspired to rush right out and find a few enemies to greet and bow to. *Thou art weighed in the balance and found wanting!* I thought of candidates. (There are times when being a minister in the starchy, judgmental Protestant tradition, rather than a guru in the Hindu tradition, suits me just fine!)

Well, okay, says God. You don't have an altar and you don't have to bow, but isn't it written somewhere in that Book (the one to which ministers in the Protestant traditions are meant to pay attention) that a truly loving person will pray for her enemies?

God can be a real pest sometimes.

However dismissive some might be of science as an alternative means of seeking or defining truth, we ministers are generally quick to seize on scientific facts if they serve our purposes or strike our fancy. (See Chapter 19, for example.)

One day an eager minister offered this one: "Did you know," he said, "that *every bit of air* on our planet gets recycled? That means that you and I have almost certainly taken into our lungs the *very same air* that kept Adam and Eve alive, that King David breathed, and that Jesus himself once drew into his blessed lungs over two thousand years ago!"

Everyone in the pews inhaled deeply.

I inhaled deeply.

Of course, Hitler breathed this air, too, I thought, and immediately, reflexively, blew out all the air as if it were toxic, and didn't inhale again until I had to.

Childish, I know: The minister wasn't trying to claim that Jesus' purity was floating around, breathable, like an airborne virus, only that we are all connected to each other and to him. Sweet . . . but there are people I don't want to be connected to. I don't want to acknowledge our common humanity, don't want to have to think about their childhood, don't even want to breathe the air that has made the journey in and out of their wretched nostrils.

"We have to have compassion, we have to understand what drove them to this," a woman said of the hijackers. "We have to *forgive!*"

It was the evening of 9/11. We had gathered at church to sing hymns and offer prayers. In New York, the rubble was still burning, and a field in Pennsylvania was wreathed in smoke. Survivors and bodies were still being pulled from the Pentagon. We didn't know what the death toll would prove to be and thus could not know the full scope of the crimes the hijackers would need to be forgiven for.

Not only was I far too angry to even think about forgiving the hijackers, I was angry with the woman for suggesting it. Wasn't she who wanted us to waste our compassion trying to understand the motives of Mohammad Atta the same woman who has a bumper sticker on her car that says, THERE'S NO EXCUSE FOR DOMESTIC VIOLENCE? Why excuse mass murderers and not wife beaters?

Clearly, I'm the last person to suggest that you build an altar in your house and put a picture of Osama bin Laden, your local wife beater, or your ex-spouse on it; nor am I about to claim that if you were a truly moral person, you would have already understood and forgiven all of these people and Hitler, too, by now.

Ram Dass didn't claim to have *forgiven* Caspar Weinberger, if it comes to that, and he certainly didn't claim to *like* him. He was willing—and only just, as he made disarmingly clear—to pray for him.

My first husband, Drew, had decided that, upon retirement from the Maine State Police, he would be ordained as a minister. Taking his calling with characteristic seriousness, he sent away for an application to the Bangor Theological Seminary, gathered and eagerly read books about theology and spirituality, and set himself a distinctive and challenging spiritual practice. "Every time I pass the state prison," he told me, "I say a prayer for the well-being of the prisoners."

At the time, the Maine State Prison was located in Thomaston, the town where we lived, so Drew passed the prison nearly every day.

"That seems awfully demanding," I said dubiously. "I mean, there are some really terrible people in there. There are murderers, child abusers, rapists, cop killers . . . and you've seen their victims. I've never had to view the aftermath of a crime, and even I would have a hard time requesting blessings for a bunch of criminals."

"It's a stretch," Drew admitted.

"Why not begin with the minimum-security facility?" I suggested. "Start with the guys who write bad checks and work your way up to the murderers and rapists?"

But Drew was never one to back down from a challenge. Day after day he drove his cruiser past the Maine State Prison and offered his prayers for mercy and healing to the high brick walls. "It really is hard," he confessed. "Still, sometimes I do at least *begin* to experience compassion for the prisoners inside."

"Love your enemies and pray for those who persecute you," Jesus of Nazareth advised.

Whom should I be praying for? Whomever is hardest to pray for, I suppose: People who have hurt me personally, people who continue to hurt me or who have hurt people I care about.

But I'm not that kind. When my dentist mentioned that my ex-boyfriend was due to have a cavity filled, I replied, "Be stingy with the Novocain." However, I'm a religious person who makes a career out of telling other people how to be moral. So I should be able to do this small thing, shouldn't I? Pray for my ex-boyfriend?

I give it a whirl. *God bless my ex*, I begin, and stop.

Problem? asks God.

To be perfectly honest, I'd rather you didn't bless him, I confess. *I'd sort of rather you smote him a little. Maybe dashed his head against a stone.*

I say unto you . . . pray for those who persecute you, says God. *And get a wiggle on.* Yeesh, what a noodge!

Okay, okay, okay . . . Just give me a minute here . . . I take a deep breath (of Jesus' air and Hitler's air). Then I say the following very fast:

God bless Charlie, and may his heart be whole. Amen.
That wasn't so bad, was it?
Yes, I say. *Thank you.*

Jesus of Nazareth made it as clear as he possibly could: "When I was hungry, you fed me . . . when I was in prison, you visited me." There is no separation: Loving God means feeding the hungry, giving drink to the thirsty, clothing the naked, attending the sick, and visiting the imprisoned.

It's a short list but a tall order. Without violating the spirit of Jesus' directive, we could add on more acts of loving kindness: comforting mourners, protecting the helpless, evacuating the stranded, adopting the orphans . . .

Jesus was a general practitioner when it came to love. The rest of us tend to specialize. For instance, I offer comfort to that particular subset of mourners whose friends and family members have perished in the woods and waters of Maine, and I support the work of game wardens doing their best to protect the helpless and evacuate the stranded.

When I mention that I work with wardens, many people assume I am a prison chaplain. I quickly disabuse them: I do not work in prisons. "I work with defenders, not offenders," I quip.

As it happens, my psychiatrist friend Diane does work with offenders, providing psychiatric and counseling services at the Maine State Prison. Not long ago she called me to request a favor. She had planned a service for inmates who had lost loved ones. The prison chaplain couldn't make it. Might I be willing to step in and take his place?

"I'm a law-enforcement chaplain, Diane," I told her. "And a police officer's widow."

"You're a minister," she said.

"Yeah, but I minister to cops. I don't do criminals."

Diane persisted. She had been leading this bereavement group for some time, and the suffering, she said, was real. "When a man's mother died, for example," she said, "not only was he not able to be with her before she died, he couldn't even attend his mother's funeral."

"Huh," I said.

"Many of them miss that all-important ritual farewell. So we are going to make this an all-inclusive memorial service," Diane explained. "I was hoping you could participate. I know you would do a beautiful job."

"I'm sure I'll be too busy."

" 'When I was imprisoned, you visited me,' " Diane quoted slyly.

It's not as if I'd never been in a prison. I've had reason to hang around local lockups and county jails in the line of my duty. Also, before the state tore down the old state prison in Thomaston, they held an open house so that any citizen who wanted to could tour the place while it was there, standing empty.

Naturally, we went. So did thirty thousand other people, at least a few of whom were obviously alumni, bringing Mom and Dad along on a nostalgic visit. They showed off the cells where they'd done their time, posed with their hands on the bars so Mom could take a photo.

I wasn't allowed to bring anything into the new maximum-security prison other than my driver's license and car keys, both of which were surrendered to an all but invisible guard behind a thick panel of smoked bulletproof glass. In return, I received an identification tag (VISITOR) and a man-down device, a thing about the size and weight of an iron BlackBerry. In the top, a peg was held in place by gravity. If I were to be threatened, I could pull the peg, and if I were knocked to the ground, it would fall out by itself, an alarm would sound, and guards would come running.

Diane breezily explained all of this as we passed through the metal detectors and then through the first of several sets of heavy doors that closed with a dramatic clang behind us.

The memorial service was held in a large room at the center of the prison. The room's walls were made of cinder blocks, and large windows on all sides permitted the guards and other prisoners to watch the mourners gather. The bereaved were in their usual attire: gray sweatpants and a white T-shirt with a large plastic identification card clipped to the chest.

I was wearing a black suit and a clerical collar and might have looked reasonably dignified, I suppose, except that the name tag was bunching my jacket and the man-down device was dragging my pants off my hips.

The prisoners stole surreptitious looks at me as they took their seats in rows of plastic chairs. I hitched at my pants and stole surreptitious looks at them, too. *They look so ordinary,* I thought. *Like a convention of car salesmen—or clergy, for that matter.*

Diane had told me there were serious offenders in the group, men who had committed violent acts, though she hadn't specified what kind.

I'll have to ask Diane not to mention that I'm a law-enforcement chaplain. Actually, I would be more comfortable if she didn't use my last name or suggest that I might be local. These guys are going to get out one day.

Diane was engaged in a last-minute consultation with one of the inmate-organizers of the event, a man who, unlike most of the others, really did look like a convict. His head was shaved, and his standard-issue T-shirt sleeves were tightly stretched over vast arms covered entirely with lurid tattoos.

I sat down in a folding chair and waited, nervously folding and refolding the paper that held my selection of bland ecumenical prayers.

When they had finished their conversation, the enormous tattooed convict came over and sat down beside me, and Diane marched briskly to the front of the room. "We can only be here for an hour," she said loudly, placing two large plastic diaper-wipe containers—one filled with flowers, one empty—on the table. "So let's get started."

She offered opening remarks, describing the prison's bereavement support program and praising the inmates' open and honest participation. Then the enormous tattooed man read some poems he'd penned while in solitary confinement, and a weedy little fellow with thick glasses and protuberant front teeth read a letter to his dead sister. Then each mourner was encouraged to come forward, select a flower from the container, and say the name of his departed loved one.

My mom got cancer . . .

My baby daughter died in her crib . . .

My dad, back in 'Nam . . .

My brother Joey was killed in an accident . . .

Gram and Granddad, both of 'em, in March . . .

My ex-wife . . .

One diaper-wipe container slowly emptied of blossoms, and the other slowly filled. The voices went on, some clear, some halting, others ragged with grief. One man broke down altogether, and the tattooed poet put his enormous arms around him.

When at last the litany of names ended, I rose, and Diane leaped forward to introduce me. "Reverend Kate Braestrup is a minister here in the Midcoast," she announced gaily. "She also serves as chaplain to our law-enforcement community! It's such a *special treat* to have Kate as our pastor today!"

From the looks on their faces, the prisoners did not seem to regard me as a special treat. Moreover, now that they knew I was, in effect, a cop, the assembled mourners looked to me a lot more like criminals.

We confronted each other across a sudden stark divide.

"It's a stretch," I could hear Drew saying.

I put down my written prayers. "Good morning," I said. "I am Reverend Kate Braestrup. I serve as chaplain to the Maine Warden Service, and my late husband, Drew, was a Maine state trooper."

I reached out and plucked one of the few remaining blossoms from the vase and held it. "On Monday, the fifteenth of April, 1996, Drew got into his cruiser and started the engine. Turning right at the bottom of the driveway, he headed south through spring sunlight. In a few minutes, he reached the Maine State Prison. He offered prayers that God's mercy and forgiveness be granted to the men imprisoned there. Those were his last prayers. A few minutes later, Drew was killed in a car accident."

I added my flower to the ones already crowding the other plastic container. "Join me, as you will, in a spirit of prayer," I said. The prisoners bowed their heads.

After we prayed, we heard music from a guitar quartet. They played extremely well. "Plenty of time to practice," one of the guitarists said ruefully when I complimented him. During a rather rushed reception, between bites of Chips Ahoy, he confided that they were trying to come up with a new name for their group. "We used to call ourselves the Three Strikes Law, but now we're a quartet, so that doesn't really work."

"How about Playing with Conviction?" I said, and he and I both laughed.

Before the Chips Ahoy and the conversation, and just before Diane rose for the last time and told us all to go in peace, the four guitar players lowered their eyes and plucked a melancholy tune from their strings. Their voices joined into effortless, heartbreaking harmony: "If the sun refused to shine, I would still be loving you."

The song is by Led Zeppelin, but I didn't know that. All I knew was that within thirty seconds of the first plangent chord, the enormous tattooed poet beside me, the weedy fellow mourning his sister, and all the men behind and around me were crying, and I was crying, too. Bright and blurry on the table before us was the yellow diaper-wipe container with all those flowers, including mine: my loss taking its place amid all those losses, Drew's prayers coming to rest at last among the men for whom he had so bravely and lovingly offered them.

Oh my God, I thought. *Oh my God.*

The tattooed guy gave me a Kleenex. I snuffled my thanks.

22

Interrupting Life for Prayer

[A lawyer] asked Jesus: "And who is my neighbor?"

Jesus replied, "A man was going down from Jerusalem to Jericho, and fell into the hands of robbers, who stripped him, beat him, and went away, leaving him half dead.

"Now by chance a priest was going down that road; and when he saw him, he passed by on the other side. So likewise a Levite, when he came to the place and saw him, passed by on the other side. But a Samaritan while traveling came near him; and when he saw him, he was moved with pity. He went to him and bandaged his wounds, having poured oil and wine on them. Then he put him on his own animal, brought him to an inn, and took care of him.

"The next day he took out two denarii, gave them to the innkeeper, and said, 'Take care of him; and when I come back, I will repay you whatever more you spend.' Which of these three, do you think, was a neighbor to the man who fell into the hands of the robbers?"

He said, "The one who showed him mercy."

Jesus said to him, "Go and do likewise."

I am blessed with a wonderful set of clergy friends, drawn from a wide variety of denominations and traditions and from all over the country. Thanks to the Internet, I am able to exploit them ruthlessly and with persistence whenever I have a problem, puzzle, or question relating to my work.

Recently, I sent around an e-mail:

> Here's a question for y'all. Let's say you're halfway through an important church service, and right in the middle of a terrific sermon. Suddenly, someone in the congregation gets sick. Really sick, that is: a possible heart attack, stroke, or seizure. Something serious.
>
> Useful people rush over to render appropriate medical care, an ambulance is called, the afflicted person is bundled out of the sanctuary, and the doors close behind him.
>
> What do you do then?

This had happened at a baccalaureate service for a graduating high school class in our area. Halfway through the sermon, one of the graduating girls had a seizure. There were six doctors and three nurses in the crowd of family members, so she was well taken care of. Indeed, with assistance, she was able to walk out of the sanctuary to where the ambulance was waiting. The doors closed behind her.

Then the sermon and the service went on exactly as before.

There were five clergypersons presiding (a Catholic priest, a rabbi, and three Protestants: Baptist, Methodist, and Congregational), and I kept waiting for someone to say something along the lines of "Don't worry, children. Our friend is going to be all right. Capable people are taking good care of her. So let's take a moment in prayer together, asking that God lend courage to her heart and skill and strength to those who would heal her."

One Sabbath day, Luke tells us, Jesus was on his way to the house of a leader of the Pharisees for supper. He happened upon a man who had a painful and debilitating condition now known by the term "edema" (a pathological retention of lymphatic fluid between the tissues of the body). Jesus asked the lawyers and the Pharisees, "Is it lawful to cure people on the Sabbath or not?" They were silent. So Jesus healed the man there and then. Then he asked, "If one of you had a child or an ox that has fallen into a well, wouldn't you pull it out on the Sabbath day?"

All the clergy involved in the service are good people, so maybe I'm just a little too chaplain-esque to understand the requirements of church decorum. But isn't this one of those moments when you must let the important thing go, at least long enough to do the Really Important Thing?

"I am aghast," one Baptist minister responded, and that pretty much summed up the e-mail consensus. In a variety of ways, expressive of the various theologies my friends hold dear, they all said they would have stopped the service and said a prayer, and most of them related their experiences of having to do exactly that. One reported that a death had occurred—it could happen as easily in church as anywhere—and of course the original service was set aside completely.

Following the terrorist attacks of September 11, many heretofore unobservant Americans felt compelled to find a sanctuary where they might share their sorrow and rage and join with others in prayer. Rabbis, priests, imams, and pastors all over the country had to set aside their original plans for the weekly service, write a whole new sermon, and select different hymns in response.

I do know at least one minister who insisted that his sermon of September 16, 2001, would be and should be the same. I think his rationale was that the best thing we could do for ourselves would be to carry on normally, and changing the service would be an overreaction.

Maybe. But I wonder how many people arrived in the pews before his pulpit that day heartbroken and yearning—and departed heartbroken, yearning, and resolved never to set foot in church again.

I wonder how many of the graduates at the baccalaureate service simply concluded (despite the minister's humor and his hip way of quoting rock lyrics) that religion, clergy, church, hymns, prayers, even God, had nothing to do with them, nothing to do with life.

Protestant traditions have what is known as the Priesthood of All Believers, a principle that argues we are all, in effect, called to be ministers—givers of care and *locum tenens* (placeholders) for God.

So let's say you're at a meeting of your book club, Rotary Club, or Neighborhood Watch group, and someone is stricken with a serious medical condition. Those who can offer practical compassion should be given room to do so. Once that part is past and everyone has settled uncertainly back in their seats, you can stand up and say:

"Excuse me . . . excuse me? *YO!* I need to say something before we go on with the meeting. Would everyone here please allow me to offer a moment's prayer for [insert name]? God lend courage to [name's] heart, and skill and strength to those who would heal her. Amen."

"Thank you. I feel better."

You can do this. Fear not. (Remember: The egg must break before the bird can fly, and today is only the tomorrow you worried about yesterday.) You really will feel better, and everyone else in the room will feel better, too.

I was going to qualify that statement by saying "almost everyone else in the room," but there is no need. *Everyone* in the room will feel stronger, more loving, more connected, and better able to go forward (I promise).

23

Refraining

This should be obvious, but shouting out a psalm of triumphant thanksgiving at the funeral of a business rival is not just inappropriate—it isn't a prayer, no matter how many times the speaker utters the name of God.

Revenge, ghoulish satisfaction, and schadenfreude, however justified they might feel under your particular set of circumstances, are not love. Love is the only legitimate intention for prayer.

Prayer can be misused. Even in my short life on earth, I have heard polemics, insults, and comedy routines offered under the guise of "prayer."

Don't get me wrong: I like political speeches and polemics, I do occasionally yield to the impulse to insult somebody (usually a relative), and I love a good joke. But if we are to allow that prayer has any power at all, we have to be very clear about what we're doing, and what we definitely should not be doing, once we have invoked that power.

As a minister, I bear a far heavier responsibility for maintaining clarity about such things than a layperson. Week after week, a little congregation in Pittsfield, Maine, sits quietly in the pews and allows me, a mere student, to occupy a raised pulpit and speak on behalf of all that is holy. The widower of a suicide turns his sorrowing eyes to me and asks me to pray with him. Or a bereaved mother, or a son grieving the death of his father.

My power arises directly out of the trust other people give me. It is real power. I could hurt my congregants or the grief-stricken badly were I to misuse it. Ultimately, there is no such thing as power without responsibility.

Religious language is powerful language, even in a secular society.

When the Reverend Billy Graham spoke at the National Day of Prayer on September 14, 2001, he preached a warm, generous sermon. Addressing the theme of hope, he said the following: "Many of those people who died this past week are in heaven right now, and they wouldn't want to come back. It's so glorious and wonderful."

Afterward, I talked to a New York cop who had heard Graham say "Many of those who died this past week are in heaven" and thought: *Wait a minute.*

Many?

Not all?

"Who *isn't* in heaven?" he demanded angrily of me. "The Jewish cop, the Muslim cop, the gay cop?" It wasn't an idle matter to him. His comrades were gone; the cries of the widows rang in his ears.

It sounds picky, perhaps, but his was the objection of a person predisposed by grief to listen with unusual attention when a Man of God speaks. If God's love does speak through a clergy person, the grieving—of all people—will hear it, which makes it an extraordinary privilege to offer prayers to those who mourn.

When we are called to offer prayers, whether professionally or not, it is a good thing to declare frankly our human limitations ("I'm speaking for Christians, now," Billy Graham said, so he did try) before we pray, and we should be quick to substitute loving presence and humble silence whenever words might get in the way of love.

Despite my essentially secular upbringing, I did occasionally go to church with my grandmother. She was neither religious nor spiritual, particularly, but the summer service at the Episcopal chapel on the island of Islesboro, Maine, was de rigueur, part of the summer social scene. (This must be where I, along with my siblings and cousins, learned to say the Episcopal version of the Lord's Prayer.)

My grandmother liked the hymns, particularly the vigorous martial ones—"Onward, Christian Soldiers" and "A Mighty Fortress Is Our God." So she went to church in the summertime, but otherwise, my grandmother—known to the family as Gaga—lived a happily secular life in New York City.

When my grandmother's second husband developed Alzheimer's, it was decided that Islesboro was a friendlier place than Manhattan in which to lose one's mind. Gaga and her husband winterized their summer cottage and became year-round island residents. The summer people migrated south without them, and the Episcopal chapel closed its doors. My grandmother was a little lonely, I think, and became even more so after my step-grandfather died.

Gaga's housekeeper told her about the sewing circle at the Baptist Church. She also mentioned that the minister was handsome, and Gaga always had an eye for male pulchritude. So the next thing her family knew, Gaga had become a Baptist—sort of. She informed the attractive Reverend Bacon during his very first pastoral visit that she was an atheist. (She took care to remind him frequently.) But she joined the sewing circle, went to potluck dinners, and attended services, belting out her favorite hymns with downright evangelical vigor. On Sundays, Reverend Bacon preached about the living God. God definitely exists, he preached. God is creator, sustainer, and redeemer. God is just and righteous. God is merciful.

Incidentally, did you know that there is a problem with a God conceived of as merciful? I didn't until one day, at seminary, a professor raised the issue. "Doesn't mercy presuppose power, dominance, and even the possibility of violence?" he inquired. "The concept of mercy, after all, implies restraint, not incapacity. If God mercifully restrains God's-self from squashing us like cockroaches, aren't we grateful and moved to praise precisely because we know God is capable of doing otherwise?"

Some of my classmates found this train of thought disturbing. "We would be better off," one said, "with a God conceived of as more of an equal partner with humanity, rather than dominant over humanity." There were nods of agreement around the room: Yes, yes, that would be much better. Maybe God could be the moderator of the meeting, but we would all be present as equal stakeholders, each of us a change agent, each responsible for processing his or her own issues and for bringing the coffee and doughnuts when it was our turn.

But then some wet blanket had to remind us that we—that is, most of us (with a sidelong glance at the Unitarian Universalists in the room)—are Christians. Christians have the Bible. In the Bible, God is most definitely not an equal partner.

God makes this clear in the Book of Job: *Where were you when I laid the foundations of the earth?* God roars from the midst of a whirlwind when Job dares to complain about his troubles. *Have you walked in the depths of the sea? Can you loose the bands of Orion? Did you give the horse strength, or clothe his neck with thunder?*

"What if God was one of us? Just a slob like one of us?"

But God isn't.

God is omnipotent, omniscient, omnivorous, and all the rest of it, and humanity is limited and weak. The cosmos is not a democracy.

I will say of the Lord He is my refuge and my fortress, the psalmist declares. *He shall cover me with his feathers, under his wings shall I trust; his truth shall be my shield and buckler. I shall not be afraid for the terror by night nor the arrow that flieth by day. Nor for the pestilence that walketh in darkness, nor for the destruction that wasteth at noonday.*

God as architecture, God as mother hen, God as body armor, God as Tamiflu: In the Bible, the power of God is an antidote to our mortal vulnerability to natural disaster and human aggression.

If God is just a slob like one of us, God can't be a mighty fortress. A God imagined as the equal of humanity, ready to offer warm fuzzies but not protection, empathy but no particular wisdom, would be useless for a vulnerable people.

On the other hand, if God is powerful enough to squash the enemies of the faithful in some satisfactorily violent and final manner, God will also, by definition, be capable of squashing the faithful themselves. God's power is a double-edged sword. Mercy is what keeps God's sharp edge from striking us.

Sitting in that seminary classroom, I was visited by a not uncommon smugness. I am a Unitarian Universalist, the most liberal of the liberal faiths. So I'm not saddled with the Omni-God. A representative government with its armies and police will protect me from mine enemies, and antibiotics will protect me from plagues. God *can* be one of us, just a slob like one of us: This merciful, powerful God is really not my problem.

Then pipes up that still, small, irritating voice: *But is the problem of power and mercy truly not your problem, Kate? You who work with police officers, men and women bearing the power of life and death on their all too human hips?*

Ours is a world filled with asymmetrical power relationships, the human-divine being only one of these. The ancients understood this. While they clearly hoped to be the beneficiaries of God's mercy, they didn't think of mercy as an expression of a disproportionate and therefore intrinsically illegitimate power. When my professor suggested that mercy exposed the problem implicit in the theological concept of an omnipotent God, he was speaking from a distinctly modern, American perspective.

Our modern, democratic state exists because our enlightened forebears finally twigged to the calamitous effects of disproportionate power in political arrangements and—bravo!—asserted that all men are created equal. Extending the principle, we no longer accept whites' power over nonwhites or male power over women. It has recently become fashionable to deplore, and even seek legal remedy for, asymmetrical power in parent-child relationships.

My daughter Woolie and I, for example, are in an asymmetrical power relationship. Woolie is more ignorant. I outweigh her by about fifty pounds. I have all the money.

We are also unequal in that I am responsible for her well-being, while she is not responsible for mine. She doesn't have to defend me. My power and strength exist so that I can defend her. To be her mighty fortress is a duty engraved into my very bones: I have to keep her from starving, from playing with matches, from failing at school, from smoking pot. I work hard at these things. If Woolie were to bring home a report card full of Fs, an unsuitable boyfriend, or a metal spike through her eyebrow, then, like the God of the Prophets, I would doubtless cry, *O faithless daughter! Has counsel perished from the prudent? Has your wisdom vanished? Flee, turn back, get down low . . . For I will bring the calamity upon you!*

One of the recurring metaphors for the powerful God of the Bible is that of a divine parent. Parents have power. If a parent, divine or otherwise, is a good parent, he or she will eventually stop spluttering and hollering. She will mete out appropriate consequences—we won't call them punishments—until the child appears to be appropriately contrite, and then the parent will be merciful.

Woolie is a child. I assume less control over her life now than I did when she was an infant. Indeed, parenting can be described as a process wherein power shifts by slow but steady increments from parent to child as the child grows and becomes ever more responsible for herself.

Here, by the way, is where the parental metaphor for God begins to break down: We never grow up! God is never done! Can you imagine? All God wants is to take a shower by Herself, maybe enjoy an uninterrupted conversation with Her friend Mother Teresa, and She's got these human beings, perpetual adolescents, demanding and complaining forever and ever, world without end . . .

The parental metaphor for God highlights the relationship

between power and responsibility. In God's case, among all those other omnis, God is omni-responsible. This is God's world. God created it, God sustains it, and only God can redeem it. There are no equal partners. Whatever happens or doesn't, it's God's gig.

The parental metaphor also highlights the crucial, legitimating role of love.

I have been entrusted with incredible power and awesome responsibility when it comes to Woolie and her siblings. The asymmetry of power and responsibility in our relationship is not an end in itself but a means to the only holy end of human endeavor, which is love. That's why parenting doesn't feel like power. That's why it feels like service.

Whatever God is or is not, asymmetrical power relationships do exist, naturally and unavoidably, among human beings. Most of us have some kind of power that we exercise over others, even as others exercise theirs over us. This is inevitable and important. Think not only of the necessary power of parents over children but of cops over citizens—do you really want a cop who claims no more than an equal partnership with you when a murderer is breaking down the door? Do you want your heart surgeon to give you a turn with the scalpel? How can we loose the fetters of injustice if we consider ourselves equally oppressed or no more than equally free?

There are the powers of the beautiful and the talented, and the powers of those who can speak in the tongues of mortals and of angels, prophetic powers and the understanding of mysteries; there are those who can move mountains. None of these powers can be practically or morally renounced. Whatever power you possess, you're stuck with it. The most you can do is pretend to be powerless. (I've known parents who try this. I feel sorry for their children.)

"When I became a cop, I thought the job would be all about power," a friend once told me. "Then I found out it is all about service. And I found out I really liked it that way."

Power can be abused. If power can't be abused, it isn't power.

Still, my power and yours, whatever yours consists of, can be redeemed and made righteous by mercy. Mercy is what we call it when power is exercised and restrained for the sake of love.

My grandmother, as I said, became an atheist Baptist in the last years of her life. Sunday after Sunday, she listened to Reverend Bacon's sermons about the power and mercy of God and sang the hymns with vigor.

Then her health began to fail. It failed some more, and then some more, and at last my grandmother knew the end was coming. So she took the ferry over to the mainland and checked herself in to the local hospital. She told her physician she was quite aware she was about to die and wished for no heroic lifesaving measures, only for sufficient morphine to keep her out of pain. (She was very specific about the morphine. Gaga had always wanted to try morphine.)

Then Gaga changed into her rose-printed flannel nightie and climbed into bed. Dying took about a week. Her children—my mother, aunts, and uncle—arrived to attend to her in shifts around the clock.

One day—the next-to-last day, as it turned out—two of my aunts were standing in the hallway outside Gaga's hospital room when a handsome man arrived. He introduced himself as Gaga's pastor.

My aunts—reared, after all, to be summer Episcopalians and Manhattan atheists—didn't know what to make of him. They didn't want this Baptist person to confront Gaga at a vulnerable moment and shove a lot of religious fiddle-faddle down her throat when she could no longer defend herself. But they didn't quite know how to refuse him entry, either.

So Reverend Bacon entered the hospital room where my grandmother lay dying and closed the door behind him. It wasn't until after the funeral that the family found out what happened in there.

My grandmother looked up and saw Reverend Bacon. She was too weak to speak, but she briefly raised her hand from the bedspread.

Reverend Bacon sat down beside her on the bed. He asked her, "Would you like me to pray with you?"

And something in her face . . . *something in her face!* . . . told him no.

So he sat beside her for an hour and simply held her hand.

Now, I know it is possible that Reverend Bacon had never done a good thing before this moment. It's possible that he hasn't done any good things since. I doubt both propositions, but even if both were proved true, I would tell you that to me this one delicate, restrained act, an act of perfect mercy, justifies his title and his power as a Man of God.

If I speak in the tongues of mortals and of angels, but do not have love, I am a noisy gong or a clanging cymbal, St. Paul wrote to the Christians at Corinth. *And if I have prophetic powers, and understand all mysteries and all knowledge, and if I have all faith, so as to remove mountains, but do not have love, I am nothing.*

God—even in the Bible—isn't defined by His power, though the God of the Bible is powerful.

The insight of the Jewish and Christian traditions is that, while there is disproportionate power in the world, this is a reality we will not escape. Yet the tradition insists upon an accompanying magnificent claim: That power is nothing, *nothing,* unless it is merciful. Unless, that is, it is turned always to the service of love.

O Lord, what are human beings that you regard them . . . They are like a breath; their days are like a passing shadow. Bow your heavens, O Lord, and come down, the psalmist cries. And God, in God's power and in God's mercy, comes down.

PART SIX

Leap

24

Faith

My stepdaughter Ilona is at Hartwick College now, majoring in nursing and working hard to make herself into one of Love's most useful practical tools. I went to visit, and Ilona showed me around the nursing school, which boasts a spiffy replica of a typical hospital ward with all the accoutrements: johnny gowns, drawsheets, bedpans, charts, catheters, monitors, IV poles, those trapezes that bedbound patients can hold on to when they want to change position, and mechanical beds—neatly made, with hospital corners and electric controls that make them go up and down. In one bed, I saw a figure resting quietly: It was a medical dummy. Caucasian, male, and remarkably realistic, he bore with plastic patience a Joblike plethora of unpleasant plastic maladies. An IV needle was planted in his forearm, and a chemotherapy port gaped in his chest; he had a urinary catheter, a colostomy, a bedsore, a surgical wound, and, for all I know, a fish bone stuck in his throat.

I knew the patient for the object it was: I wasn't fooled. But the poor, afflicted dummy provoked a kind of chaplain's reflex, an all but irresistible urge to go over, take the dummy's plastic hand between my own, and tenderly inquire whether he might like a word of prayer.

* * *

My friend James Weathersby is African-American. When he prays, he tells me, "I stand on the shoulders of countless generations of my family who prayed for me to have a better life than they did during the Middle Passage, slavery, Jim Crow, legalized segregation, and discrimination."

A pastor and chaplain, James serves in a hospital for people who are severely, even criminally, mentally ill. "Prayer is dynamic and powerful; it changes me or changes how I see things around me," he says.

James is also—indeed, primarily—an attentive and loving man. "The privilege of prayer never escapes me," he says.

In her poem "Wild Geese," the poet Mary Oliver reassures us that we needn't "walk on our knees for a hundred miles through the desert, repenting."

You can just allow your body to arrange itself in surrender and allow yourself to yield before all that is vast, incomprehensible, and stronger by far than your own soft self.

"Prayer, for me, is commonplace," my friend Jackie says. "I pray every day, usually before bed at night. I pray for the health and welfare of my family. I pray for protection, peace, and prosperity. I pray for direction and help in everything that I do . . . I pray for blessings so that I may be a blessing to others. I pray because I know that God hears me and he answers."

Or, as the psalmist puts it:

You are my refuge and my strength
A very present help in trouble
Therefore, I shall not fear, though
The earth should change, though the mountains
Shake in the heart of the sea; though the waters roar and foam . . .
Psalm 46:1–3 (adapted)

Whether I have faith or not, am mindful or oblivious, whether I scatter stones or gather them together, God will be just exactly what God is. Or isn't. Whatever the reality of God is, you and I have neither the power nor the responsibility for creating, sustaining, or redeeming it.

So let's be clear, as President Obama would say: Faith is not the confidence that my religious views are true and correct in every jot and tittle. It is not the assurance that, because God loves me, nothing bad is going to happen to me or to those I love.

Faith is, rather, knowing that there is a goodness and rightness in the world that is of God: a righteous, grand, and holy love that I will never wholly grasp but in which I am invited to participate through the giving and receiving of human love.

Faith is the confidence that no matter what happens, love is always available—as action, as memory, as a gift from others, as a capacity in myself.

If God is love, then what my faith requires is that I notice the love in which I move and breathe and have my being, love at work in my world, in my species (Pan sapiens, Homo caritans) and in myself. And so I pray. *Yes. Wow. Thank you.*

On a gloomy November day not long ago, I drove to Augusta for an afternoon meeting. The low winter sun painted the passing landscape in a range of grays and sere browns: gray sky, brown trees, brown fields bleached cold, ochre by frost. In Maine the cold and dark loom so absolutely that anyone with a human soul yearns for warmth and radiance. I felt my kinship with all the ancient peoples who regarded the increasingly brief and pallid visits of the winter sun with anxiety.

I cranked up the heat, even though the air inside the car was warm. I fretted about the cost of oil (*Oh, God!*) and whether we would be able to cut and stack more firewood before the snows came.

I planned some panicked knitting: sweaters, socks, leg warmers, mittens, and hats! *Maybe if I encase my loved ones entirely in wool, they will survive the winter?*

A farm borders the road in the town of Union, and as I passed the place, I glimpsed a scene with plenty of biblical antecedents: a flock of sheep abiding in a pasture. Some lay on the ground, padded from its stone frozen hardness by thick fleece. Others clustered around a pile of hay.

On the backs of some of the ewes, I noticed a streak of color, blue or red, as if a toddler had been let loose among them with a couple of giant crayons. Even before I had retrieved the memory of what those streaks of color signified, I felt the stirring of faith. Even before I'd figured the thing out, I was grinning at the darkening sky beyond my windshield.

Yes, the winter has come, I thought, *but spring—even in Maine—will surely follow.*

In the early 1970s, my parents bought a farm in the mountains of Maryland. There, my mother kept a flock of sixty sheep. Most were ewes, of the breed known as Corriedales, but Mom also kept two rams. One was a huge, solid, black-headed beast with a Roman nose and an imperturbable disposition. He was known simply as Big John. The other ram was a slight, skinny creature, a Cheviot. He looked quite a lot like Gene Wilder with his wild, curly hair; he also had yellow eyes that didn't quite track. This animal Mom christened Sauerkraut.

Sauerkraut spent most of his life hovering on the brink of a nervous breakdown. A laughing child, a duck's quack, and even blowing leaves could startle Sauerkraut into a frenzy of bleating and directionless stampede. Any more substantial threat—a barking dog or the arrival of the vet—would completely freak him out. If ever a sheep needed Valium, it was Sauerkraut. Sauerkraut was also terrified of Big John, and this made for peace in the sheepfold for most of the year.

Once a year, however, in late autumn, it would be time for the ewes to be bred. What signal passed from the ewes, or from the gods of ovine reproduction, into the twitching convolutions of Sauerkraut's tiny brain, I do not know. But as the leaves changed color, the flame of some unnamable passion would flare up in Sauerkraut's heart, and a change would come over him. Instead of cowering in the corner of the sheepfold, trying to keep a couple dozen ewes between him and various imaginary dangers, Sauerkraut would begin to strut and swagger about on his scrawny legs. If any blowing leaves or quacking ducks happened across his path, Sauerkraut would snort in a threatening manner, then steal a quick glance at the ewes to see if they noticed his bravery.

The ewes would go on clipping at the grass with their front teeth, paying no attention at all to Sauerkraut. Their indifference would drive him to more dramatic displays of machismo. Lowering his head, he would charge at the dogs, who ran barking, laughing, out of his way. And still the ewes grazed, impervious.

His soul on fire, Sauerkraut would draw a deep and desperate breath, and from the recesses of his scrawny chest would come a prolonged, savage snort of challenge. Okay, it sounded more like a savage squeak of challenge, but no matter. It had the desired effect.

Big John's black head would pop up above the woolly surface of the flock. He would turn his steely gaze in Sauerkraut's direction and emit a more resonant, answering snort, the ovine equivalent of "You talking to *me*, boy?

Sauerkraut would reply with his shrill squeak: "You bet I am! Big Nose!"

The flock of ewes would part like the Red Sea before the upraised hand of Moses, leaving the ground between the two rams clear and empty. A hush would fall over the sheepfold as ewes and lambs, ducks and dogs held their breath.

THUD! THUD! Big John would stomp his front feet upon the ground.

Thud! Thud! An answering signal from Sauerkraut, whose expression (insofar as sheep are capable of expression) was resolute. He would not yield.

Big John lowered his massive head.

Sauerkraut lowered his tiny head, his curls shivering in the wind.

And then, as if on some silent signal sharp as a gunshot, the rams charged. WHOMP! Their heads collided.

I would love to be able to surprise you at this point.

But I can't. The result was exactly as you would predict. Sauerkraut would promptly fall over onto his back, all four feet in the air, just like a cartoon, with little Xs where his eyes should be, and Big John would amble away to resume eating, completely unaffected.

The injury wasn't fatal. Sauerkraut would eventually open one eye and then the other. He'd get to his feet and totter about in a daze for several hours until his head cleared sufficiently to think about demanding a rematch.

In truth, the flock of ewes was not a prize for Big John or Sauerkraut to win or lose by any display of foolishness or courage. My mother, goddess of the sheepfold, would divide the flock into roughly equal groups of ewes, one for Sauerkraut (whose curly wool was prized for spinning) and one for the meaty Big John.

Both rams would be fitted out with harnesses that held chalk—blue chalk for Big John, red for Sauerkraut. When a mating had been accomplished, Mom would see the mark on the ewe's back and note the date in her record book. Thus, she could roughly calculate when a birth might reasonably be expected.

Lambs were the first sign of spring on our farm. They would be born, scrawny and steaming, into the freezing February nights. It always seemed impossible that anything so small and wet could survive birth into such conditions. Some didn't, and that was sad, but most of them did. They would stagger to their soft feet, find their mother's milk, and drink. Soon enough, they would grow fat and silly, leaping in the warm air, nibbling experimentally at the new grass in the fresh spring light. Some would have a black face and a Roman nose. Others would have curly hair and yellow eyes that did not quite track.

There were sheep in the fields in Union, Maine, and their wool bore a mark made with chalk.

It was a sign, for those who know, of a coming miracle. Spring will come, the green fields and the dancing lambs. The lambs are already on their way, just as the bulbs and seeds that shall be flowers are already waiting in the soil, and the sap rests even now in the roots of the maple trees. With the winter solstice, the earth will tilt back into the center of that blessed cone of sunlight to warm a belly already pregnant with the new spring.

My prayers cannot make the earth tilt or the sap rise, and neither the tilt nor the rise are mine. In the grand scheme of things, my faith is unnecessary, and so it comes to me as grace: *Yes! Wow. Thank you!*

Even as the darkness and the cold close in, the warmth, flowers, lambs, and light are on their way. Nothing more than time is needed for the prayers to be answered and the promise to be fulfilled.

Amen.

Appendix of Prayers

HOSPITAL PRAYER

O God, whose name is love
I offer the prayer of my yearning heart
I can't hold or heal my child.
Please, hold her for me.
Love moves in the skilled hands of those who would heal my
     baby
Love is in their learning and their care
God be in my understanding.
God be in my patience
God be in my arms, as she is returned to me.
May my child and all children be blessed
My family and all families blessed
May God's love enfold us, dwell in us, give us comfort
And grant us peace.
Amen.

      KB

PSALM 23

The Lord is my shepherd, I shall not want.
He makes me lie down in green pastures;

He leads me beside still waters;
He restores my soul
He leads me in right paths for his name's sake.

Even though I walk through the darkest valley,
I will fear no evil;
for you art with me;
your rod and your staff—
they comfort me.

You prepare a table before me
in the presence of my enemies;
you anoint my head with oil,
my cup overflows.
Surely goodness and mercy shall follow me
all the days of my life,
and I shall dwell in the house of the Lord
my whole life long.

DANISH PRAYER

Sing praises of the Lord with heart and soul
Singing heart, embrace the spirit
The notes play, like the stars that sparkle
Joyously around the name of the Lord.
N. F. S. Grunvig

FAMILY GRACE

We are thankful for the food
And for the hands that prepared it
And for our family and for our friends.
Amen.

Appendix of Prayers

TRADITIONAL GRACE

Bless us, O Lord and these thy gifts
Which we are about to receive from Thy bounty
Through Christ our Lord.
Amen.

GRACE

For the food before us
And the friends beside us
And the love that surrounds us
We are truly grateful.

FROM PSALM 147

Sing to the LORD with thanksgiving;
make melody to our God on the lyre.
He covers the heavens with clouds,
prepares rain for the earth,
makes grass grow on the hills.
He gives to the animals their food,
and to the young ravens when they cry.

TRADITIONAL GRACE SONG

Oh! The Lord is good to me
And so I thank the Lord
For giving me
The things I need
The sun and the moon and the apple tree
The Lord is good to me—YIPPEE!

SWIFT GRACE

May the hungry be well fed. May the well fed hunger for justice.
Amen.

FROM PSALM 118

This is the day that the Lord has made. Let us rejoice and be glad
in it.

BLESSING

Blessed is the spot
And the house
And the temple
And the city street
And the human heart
And the clinic
And the sidewalk
And the bridge
And the riverbank
And the refuge
And the stony beach
And the flowering orchard
And the cliff top
And the ice floe
And the barley field
And the deep woods
Blessed is the place
Where mention of God has been made
Where God's love has been offered and received

By human voices, by human ears, by blessed human hands.
Amen.

KB

TRADITIONAL CHILDREN'S BEDTIME PRAYER

Now I lay me down to sleep
I pray the Lord my soul to keep
If I should die before I wake
I pray the Lord my soul to take.

CHILDREN'S BEDTIME PRAYER (ADAPTED)

Now I lay me down to sleep
I pray that love my soul will keep
My body rest, my love expand
To every soul in every land.
God bless . . .
Amen.

AFRICAN PRAYER

God save us
God hide us.
When we sleep, God, do not sleep
If we sleep, God, do not get drowsy,
Tie us around Your arm, God,
Like a bracelet.

OLD CELTIC PRAYER

Lord and God of Power
Shield and sustain me this night.
Lord, God of Power
This night and every night.

FROM PSALM 108

Awake, my soul!
Awake, O harp and lyre!
I will awake the dawn.

ST. AUGUSTINE'S PRAYER

Watch, dear Lord, with those who wake
Or watch, or work or weep tonight,
And give your angels charge
Over those who sleep.
Tend your sick ones, O Lord God
Rest your weary ones.
Bless your dying ones.
Soothe Your suffering ones.
Pity your afflicted ones.
Shield your joyous ones.
All for your love's sake.
Amen.

Appendix of Prayers

ADULT'S BEDTIME PRAYER I

O God, I offer the prayers of my heart
May I be held in your hands as I sleep
May I be blessed by your love. May I arise with joy in the
      morning.
For those I name aloud [names],
May they be held in your hands and blessed by your love.
May they arise with joy in the morning.
For those whose names I do not know but whose sufferings I
      know to be real to you,
Help me, that they might become real to me.
May they be held in your hands and blessed by your love.
May they arise with joy in the morning.
Amen.

MARRIAGE BLESSING

May these vows and this marriage be blessed.
May this marriage be delicious milk,
Like wine and halvah.
May it offer fruit and shade
Like the date palm.
May this marriage be full of laughter
Making every day a day in Paradise
May this marriage be a token of compassion
A seal of joy now and forever more.
May this marriage have a gracious face and a good name,
An omen as welcome
As the moon in a clear, daylight sky.
I have run out of words to describe
How spirit mingles in this marriage!
      Jalal al-Din Rumi

FROM THE SONG OF SOLOMON

How fair and pleasant you are,
O loved one, delectable maiden!
You are stately as a palm tree,
and your breasts are like its clusters.
I say I will climb the palm tree
And lay hold of its branches.
Oh may your breasts be like clusters of the vine,
And the scent of your breath like apples,
Your kisses like the best wine
That goes down smoothly
Gliding over lips and teeth . . .

How graceful are your feet in sandals,
O queenly maiden!
Your rounded thighs are like jewels,
the work of a master hand.
Your navel is a rounded bowl
that never lacks mixed wine.
Your belly is a heap of wheat,
encircled with lilies . . .
O . . . wind!
Blow upon my garden
that its fragrance may be wafted abroad.
Let my beloved come to his garden,
and eat its choicest fruits.

Set me as a seal upon your heart,
as a seal upon your arm;
for love is strong as death,
passion fierce as the grave.
Its flashes are flashes of fire . . .

As an apple tree among the trees of the wood,
so is my beloved among young men.
With great delight I sat in his shadow,
and his fruit was sweet to my taste.
He brought me to the banqueting house,
and his intention toward me was love . . .
My beloved is mine and I am his . . .
"Arise, my love, my fair one, and come away . . ."

IRISH BLESSING

May the road rise to meet you,
May the wind be always at your back
May the rains fall soft upon your fields
And until we meet again
May God hold you in the palm of His hand.

God be in my head,
And in my understanding;
God be in my eyes,
And in my seeing;
God be in my mouth,
And in my speaking;
God be in my heart,
And in my thinking;
God be at my end,
And at my departing.

Sarum Primer (adapted)

Appendix of Prayers

BLESSING

May the Lord bless and keep you
May the Lord make His face to shine upon you and be gracious
     unto you
May the Lord lift up His countenance upon you
And give you peace.

BLESSING

May love and strength be in your hands (hands out, palms up)
May love and courage be in your heart (hands rest, one atop the
     other, against your chest)
May love and wisdom be in your mind (palms press against your
     forehead)
May God go with you and work through you (raise hands in the air)
Today and in all your days.
Amen.
     KB

IROQUOIS PRAYER

May all I say
And all I do
Be in harmony with thee
God within me
God beyond me
Maker of the trees.

Appendix of Prayers

RICHARD OF CHICHESTER'S PRAYER

Day by day, dear Lord,
These things I pray . . .
To see Thee more clearly,
Love Thee more dearly,
And to follow Thee more nearly,
Day by day.

MORNING PRAYER,
ADAPTED FROM PSALM 51

"Create in me a clean heart, O God; and renew a right spirit
    within me."
Let the Light that can glow gently be a searchlight
Harsh and stubborn, for the Word is simple, but the way is hard
    and I am too inclined
To think
I have already reached the place to which I have been called by
    love,
And long to be.
"Open thou my lips: and my mouth shall show forth thy praise."
Before I can distract myself with other things, before I've charmed
    myself
With pleasures, comforts, the self-convincing clamor of my Self;
That idol
Who so easily wins the substance of my worship: Scour my heart
"The sacrifices of God are a broken spirit: a broken and a contrite
    heart."
I am too smart to break, too sure for contrition, too filled
With unimaginative theories that conveniently find You in me,
    Your will
In my desires.

O blessed, jealous God, who will not suffer idols
My God, whose name is love and whose work is justice
Let the light that can glow softly be a beacon shining clear,
Let no sorrow reach my ears and find me indifferent
Let no human face come before me only to find me blind
"A broken and a contrite heart, O God, thou wilt not despise."
I am the instrument of thy labor: May your unrelenting love
Scour my heart and make me fit for thy use.
Amen.

ADAPTED FROM PSALMS 69 AND 43

O God, you know my folly
The wrongs I have done are not hidden from you.
Do not let those who hope in you
Be put to shame because of me,
O Lord God of hosts;
Do not let those who seek you be dishonored
Because of me.
Send out your light and your truth
Let them lead me
Let them bring me to your holy hill
And to your dwelling
Then I will go to the altar of God
To God my exceeding joy;
And I will praise you with the harp
O God, my God.

PRAYER FOR A GLASS HEART

Blessed is the breath of the glassblower, who
With skilled and steady exhalation
Heats the gritty solid of the heart

And with his breath expands
My heart until a wider vessel is created;
Until my heart's capacity is such
The whole world can be embraced in love. Blessed be!
Even though a heart's walls ache as they expand
Even if glass must, of necessity, grow fragile
To encompass
As it shines.
Allowing light, more light, more light:
May the glassblower breathe and breathe until
With the slightest tap my heart
Flies and shatters into sand.
Blessed be the breath of the glassblower
Craftsman of fragility
Artist of the shatter and the shine.
Amen.

      KB

BEATITUDES

Blessed are the poor, for theirs is the Kingdom of God
Blessed are those who are hungry now, for they will be filled
Blessed are those who now weep
They will laugh again.

      Luke 6:20–21

PRAYER TO BE SAID
AT THE SOUND OF A SIREN

God grant courage to those who suffer,
Strength and peace to those who help.
Amen.

Appendix of Prayers

PRAYER OF PETITION

O God I offer the prayers of my heart
For those who are suffering. I don't know their names.
You know their names, and their sufferings are real to you.
Let them become real to me. Let me know how to be with them.
If they must suffer, may they know that they are not alone.
May they be clothed with love, fed with love, warmed and
      protected by love.
May they be held in your hands and blessed in your love.
May the dead find their places in memory, may the wounded be
      healed,
May the mourners be comforted. May the morning come when
      all may arise with joy.
Amen.
     KB

TRADITIONAL VEDIC MEDITATION

Let your soul lend its ear to every cry of pain
As a lotus bares its heart to drink the morning sun
Let not the fierce sun dry one tear of pain before
You yourself have wiped it from the sufferer's eyes.
But let each burning human tear fall on your heart
And there remain, nor ever brush it off!
Until the pain that caused it is removed.

PARENT'S PRAYER I

O God be with my darling child
My dear, charming, impulsive, stormy one
Hold her for me.

Free her that she may grow;
Grow in her
That she may grow in You.
May my child be loving and beloved.
Amen.

> KB

PARENT'S PRAYER II

May you comport yourselves with dignity and treat others and
yourselves with kindness.
May you remember to say "I'm sorry" when it counts;
And "I love you" when it's hard to say, and therefore matters most.
May you both express and experience thankfulness.
May this be a life of courage, kindness, and honor. May it be a life
of joy.
Amen.

> KB

PRAYER AFTER WEEPING

O God whose work and will and very name is love we thank You
for the gift we were given in [name].
We yield with confidence to grief, knowing that pain will pass and
sorrow ends, but love does not die and will not end.
Love abides in us, around us, and beyond us, forever and ever.
Thanks be to God.
Amen.

Appendix of Prayers

FATHER MYCHAL'S PRAYER

Lord, take me where you want me to go
Let me meet whom you want me to meet
Tell me what you want me to say
And keep me out of your way.

MUHAMMAD'S EXHORTATION

What actions are most excellent?
To gladden the heart of a human being
To feed the hungry
To help the afflicted
To lighten the sorrow of the sorrowful
To remove the wrongs of the injured.
That person is most beloved of God
Who does the most good to God's creatures.

FROM PSALM 19

May the words of my mouth
And the meditations of my heart
Be acceptable to you, my Lord and my God
My strength and my redeemer.

ST. TERESA OF ÁVILA'S BLESSING

Let nothing disturb you
Let nothing frighten you
All things pass away:
God never changes

Patience obtains all things.
He who has God
Finds he lacks nothing.
God alone suffices.

THE MAGNIFICAT

My soul magnifies the Lord
And my spirit rejoices in God my savior
For He has looked with favor on the lowliness of His servant
Surely from now on all generations will call me blessed
For the Mighty One has done great things for me
And holy is His name.

Luke 1:46–49

PRAY ANYWAY

Who listens to our words when we pray? Perhaps no one.
Will our prayers be answered? Probably not.
What, then, shall we do?
Pray.
Alleluia!
Amen.

KB

THE LORD'S PRAYER AND VARIATIONS

Our Father, who art in heaven,
Hallowed be thy Name,
Thy kingdom come,
Thy will be done,
On earth as it is in heaven.

Give us this day our daily bread.
And forgive us our trespasses,
As we forgive those who trespass against us.
And lead us not into temptation,
But deliver us from evil.
For thine is the kingdom, and the power, and the glory,
Forever and ever. Amen.

Our mother, who is in heaven
Hallowed be thy name
Thy kingdom come . . .

O love that is of heaven
Hallowed be the name of love
May love's dominion come
The will of love be done
On earth as it must be in any heaven worthy of the name.

May love give us this day our daily bread
May love forgive us our trespasses as we forgive those who
        trespass against us.

May love lead us not into temptation, but deliver us from evil;
For the Kingdom, the power, and the glory belong to love
Forever and ever.
Amen.
        KB

BLESSING I

May love and strength be in my hands
May love and courage be in my heart
May love and wisdom be in my mind

May love be with me and work through me today
And in all my days.
Amen.

      KB

BLESSING II

May God bless and protect me
May God smile on me and smile through me
May God befriend me and let me be a better friend
May God make me peaceful and a maker of peace.
Amen.

      KB

PSALM 23

You are my shepherd
I shall not want
You cradle me in green pastures
You lead me beside the still waters
You return my soul to me.
You guide me in the paths of righteousness
For You are righteous
Though I walk through the valley of the shadow of death, I fear
      no evil, for You are with me;
Your rod and your staff comfort me
You spread a table before me in the presence of my enemies
You soothe my head with oil
My cup runs over
Surely goodness and mercy will follow me all the days of my life
And I will dwell in Your house forever.

RUMI'S PRAYER

Today, like every day
We wake up hollow and frightened.
Don't open the door to the study and begin reading.
Reach for a musical instrument.
Let the beauty we love be what we do
There are hundreds of ways to kneel and kiss the ground.

> Jalal al-Din Rumi

ADULT'S BEDTIME PRAYER II

No part of my body is excluded from God's compassion
And none can be withdrawn from God's service.
No part of your body is excluded from God's compassion
And none can be withdrawn from God's service.
The great commandment holds no matter where we are
I love God
I love my neighbor—You
I love, with my body and beyond my body:
O God
May whatever is done by, with, to, and through this body
Be done in love.
Amen.

> KB

FROM PSALM 139 (ADAPTED)

O Lord, thou hast searched me, and known me.
Where shall I go from thy Spirit? Or where shall I flee from thy
        presence?
If I ascend to heaven, you are there

If I make my bed in Sheol, you are there.
If I take the wings of the morning and settle at the farthest limits
    of the sea
Even there your hand shall lead me, and your right hand shall
    hold me fast
If I say "Surely the darkness shall cover me, and the light around
    me become night,"
Even the darkness is not dark to you;
The darkness and the light are both alike to thee, I am fearfully
    and wonderfully made.
For it was you who formed my inward parts
You knit me together in my mother's womb
I praise you, for I am fearfully and wonderfully made
Wonderful are your works.

FROM PSALM 46

You are my refuge and my strength
A very present help in trouble
Therefore, I shall not fear, though
The earth should change, though the mountains
Shake in the heart of the sea; though the waters roar and foam . . .
    Psalm 46:1–3

PRAYER FOR A FRIEND
STRUCK DOWN BY ILLNESS

God lend courage to the heart of our friend [name]
Skill and strength to those who would heal her.
    KB

Appendix of Prayers

FROM PSALM 91

I will say of the Lord He is my refuge and my fortress
He shall cover me with his feathers, under his wings shall I trust;
his truth shall be my shield and buckler.
I shall not be afraid for the terror by night nor the arrow that
flieth by day.
Nor for the pestilence that walketh in darkness, nor for the
destruction that wasteth at noonday.

Vaya con Dios (Go with God).

Acknowledgments

Thanks are in order for the many ways in which my ministry, my projects, and this book have been supported by my colleagues. In particular, I'd like to thank Reverend Mark Glovins, Reverend Susan Stonestreet, Pastor James Weathersby, Marie Malin, Pastor Don Williams, and Reverend David Blanchard for assistance above and beyond the call of collegial duty. At the same time, I must make it clear that none of these gifted ministers is in any way responsible for the errors (whether of theology or of plain good sense) I may have committed in these pages.

Thanks are also due to friends and relatives who have generously served as sources for prayers and thoughts on prayer, especially: Natasha Belfiore, Jackie Morgan, Elizabeth Aldrich, Annie Kiermier, Alla Renée Bozarth, Alicia Carpenter, the Ballard family and the Gallogly family, and the brothers and sisters too numerous to name who form my extended law-enforcement family. Bless you all.

While she is not an ordained minister, Thea van der Ven has spent the better part of eighty years demonstrating the power of love in a very wide variety of ways, from her work as a therapist, her advocacy on behalf of those suffering with AIDS, and as a dancer and performer. Humbly, I can add to the list: She is a cheerful champion of her newest daughter-in-law's work, offering encouragement, affection, challenge, and good humor, not to mention an extraordinary example of how to live in this world. Thank you, Thea.

About the Author

Ordained in 2004, Reverend Kate Braestrup serves as chaplain to the Maine Warden Service, and is the author of the *New York Times* bestseller *Here If You Need Me*, and *Marriage and Other Acts of Charity*. Her work has appeared in the *New York Times*, the *Boston Globe, Good Housekeeping, Reader's Digest, O, Woman's Day, More, Mademoiselle, Ms., City Paper, Hope*, and *Law and Order*.

Educated at Parsons School of Design/The New School, Georgetown University, and the Bangor Theological Seminary, Braestrup was granted an honorary doctorate from Unity College in 2010, citing her work with search and rescue teams "as they search the wild lands and fresh waters of Maine for those who have lost their way."

Braestrup delivered the invocation at the 2008 National Law Enforcement Officers Memorial vigil in Washington, D.C., to officers, families of fallen officers, and dignitaries numbering over 20,000. Now represented by Greater Talent Network, Braestrup has spoken at libraries and library associations, secondary schools, colleges and universities, and to groups of law-enforcement officers, physicians, firefighters, and clergy, and preaches regularly at Unitarian Universalist and other churches around the country.

Kate Braestrup lives in Maine with her husband, artist Simon van der Ven. Between them, they have three sons, three daughters, a daughter-in-law, and eagerly await their first grandchild.